God at Work

In these pages, Ken Costa brings to bear the experience of a varied and highly responsible professional life so as to show just how the transforming gospel is at work in the workplace. It is full of acumen, shrewdness, hopefulness – in short, it is a wise book, and a delight and profit to read.

Rowan Williams
Archbishop of Canterbury

No one is better qualified than Ken Costa to write a book like this. Throughout his rise to one of the most senior positions in the banking world, he has been an inspiration to countless Christians seeking to live out their faith in their workplaces. Ken and I met at Cambridge University where we both became Christians. He has been one of my closest friends ever since. I am so glad he has been persuaded at last to put some of his wisdom and experience into print.

Nicky Gumbel
Vicar of Holy Trinity Brompton, London
Pioneer of the Alpha course

Packed with wisdom and practical advice for the workplace – this book will inspire, stretch and challenge you.

Steve Chalke
Founder of Oasis Global & Faithworks

Ken Costa is one of the outstanding bankers of his generation who is known for the passion, creativity, leadership and strategic thinking which he brings to his professional life. He is also a person of a deep Christian faith which comes out on almost every page of this book. *God at Work* is an extraordinary account of his own personal struggles with ambition, money, relationships, success and failure. Integrating faith and work is a challenge for anyone in business, and I have no doubt that this book could transform the way you work.

Lord Griffiths of Fforestfach
Vice-Chairman, Goldman Sachs International

God at Work goes a long way in pulling down the barriers that exist between the sacred and the secular.

Ken's wide experience, from his theological training and Christian service at Holy Trinity Brompton and the Alpha programme, to his success in the world of finance, make him well qualified to write on the subject.

Can a Christian be fulfilled serving in the market place? How do 'worldly' ideals of money, success, ambition and power sit side by side with Christian virtues of love, justice, compassion and service to God?

For anyone who has sought answers to these issues or anyone who has wondered how the Christian faith can thrive in a capitalist, market-driven workplace, this book is a must read.

Pastor Agu Irukwu
Senior Pastor, Jesus House for all Nations, London

Ken Costa

God at Work

Living every day
with purpose

continuum

Continuum
The Tower Building
11 York Road
London
SE1 7NX

80 Maiden Lane
Suite 704
New York
NY 10038

www.continuumbooks.com

Unless otherwise indicated, biblical quotations are from the New International Version © 1973, 1978, 1984 by the International Bible Society. (Inclusive Language version 1995, 1996.)

Some of the people mentioned in this book have had their names changed where appropriate.

British Library Cataloguing-in-Publication Data
A catalogue record for this book is available from the British Library.

ISBN 0–8264–9634–2 (hardback)
     0–8264–9635–0 (paperback)

Typeset by Kenneth Burnley, Wirral, Cheshire
Printed and bound by 1010 Printing international Ltd

Contents

Acknowledgements

This book has had a gestation period longer than any living animal. That it has finally hit the printing press is a triumph for the many, many midwives who have struggled over the years to tease the text out of me. Because this has been such a long process, the list of those who have helped so much would require a print run in itself. Thank you to everyone who has allowed me to use their stories, who has read the manuscript, made comments, checked the sources and done the typing.

A huge thanks to: Nicky Gumbel, who was the first to press me on to paper, and who has been an example and constant encourager both as critic and loyal friend; Nicky and Sila Lee who are always there to sort out the grammar and the other important things in life; Jane Williams, Graham Tomlin and John Valentine for the theological input – the heresies are mine, but their help has been invaluable; Wesley Richards, Tricia Neill and Mark Elsdon-Dew for their extraordinary persistence and hard work in moving the project forward; Robin Baird-Smith and the

Acknowledgements

Continuum team for their early show of confidence; Jonathan Aitken whose breakfast changed the course of my thoughts; the congregation and staff of Holy Trinity Brompton, our previous vicars John Collins and Sandy Millar, Jeremy Jennings, Julia Evans and Tim Hughes, who have been constantly supportive.

This book would never have happened without the gracious firmness of the 'stalinistas', Jo Glen and Lizzy Woolf who honed the manuscript into readable text and bullied me into precision.

The patience and love of Fi, who typed the manuscript, and the endurance and ribbing of Georgina, Charles, Henry and Claudia made all the difference in getting the book done.

And above all thank you to those who have prayed with me and for me and encouraged me over the years.

I have found it so easy to forget the priorities of life and to drift with the tide of work-driven activities. Every so often during the year, I come back to the warnings and encouragements of Jesus. The reminder is so clear: 'Watch out! a man's life does not consist in the abundance of his possessions' (Luke 12:15).

To this wake-up call he urges us to 'seek first his kingdom and his righteousness and all these things will be given to you as well' (Matthew 6:33). I regard re-setting aspirations to this priority as the supreme task of our lives.

Few sayings of Jesus challenge me more than his question, which is so powerful in itself that it almost requires no answer: 'What good is it for a man to gain the whole world and yet to lose his very self?' (Luke 9:25).

Introduction

As an investment banker in the City of London, I have read the *Financial Times* and the Bible almost every day for the last 30 years. People often ask how I reconcile being a banker and a Christian. There is a widespread view that God and business simply don't mix: the competitive, cut-throat demands of the marketplace are seen as the obvious enemy of Christian compassion and love. But I have found that the God who created and sustains the world is also the God of the workplace. If the Christian faith is not relevant in the workplace, it is not relevant at all.

But where did this journey of faith start? I was born in a nominally Christian country, South Africa, and grew up in the brutally oppressive apartheid era. I became President of the Students' Union at university in Johannesburg and was active in the student protest movements against the so-called 'Christian' doctrine of apartheid, whose warped theology laid claim to biblical authority for its most vicious consequences. The cruelty of the 'separate but equal' philosophy provoked in me a burning sense of injustice. Black students were not allowed into the university or halls of residence and every form of social intercourse was cut off. Offended by such injustices carried out in the name of Christianity, I became anaesthetized to the personal claims of Christ. I thus rejected Christianity in favour of what I considered the only effective philosophy of life, and the only one that would liberate people from the intolerable inhumanity of the apartheid system: Marx's 'concept of man'.

After completing a philosophy and law degree I left South Africa, because it had become clear to me that such resistance would never bring about peaceful change without a seismic change of heart. I continued my studies in England at Cambridge University. While there, I met a number of students whose lives had been changed during a Christian mission to the university. To this day they are among my best friends. Through them I came to see that at the centre of the Christian faith there was not so much a system of thought, but rather a person, Jesus Christ, whose life, crucifixion and resurrection had brought about the only true freedom that I or anyone would ever find. One evening, alone in my room, I read Mark's Gospel (because it was the shortest). I found both the claims and character of Christ compelling and I saw in Jesus the 'free-est' person who ever lived. Previously, I had only heard short sections of the Bible read at church services. The effect of reading the whole Gospel at one sitting in a modern translation was electric. God was strangely one of us. I was struck by this picture of Christ as a human being who was committed to me. I therefore embraced the faith that I had been taught but had hitherto neglected.

This faith came alive for me after an internal struggle as to whether God would be in charge of all of my life, or only some part of it. Many people accept just enough of Christianity to be miserable. I was in that camp. The struggle encapsulated itself in a vivid image of control drawn from the very marketplace where I would spend the next 30 years: it was as if my life had shares and God wanted 100 per cent control of it. A divine tug-of-war ensued. Why would God want all of me? Could there be a joint venture? Could I carve out a special deal to suit me? What about a partnership? Was 50–50 not a good arrangement? But it became clear that *true* freedom was to be found in full surrender to the love of God. It did not come to me easily, nor at once: I got there in stages. I recall praying that God would take 51 per cent of my life – control but not whole ownership. I remember the churning and the heated deliberation within myself as this plan did not seem to achieve the desired objective. I saw then, and recognize now more fully, the arrogance of negotiating with God and the foolishness in believing I had anything to offer

God. I recall praying: 'Lord, have all of me. Only don't abandon me.' In that moment, I realized that the God who loved the entire world also loved me and would stay faithful to me, even when I was not faithful to him, as has sadly often been the case.

What struck me at once was the immediate change in every area of my life. My internal wrestling on the meaning of life ceased, peace with God and with myself grew and my life was redirected with a new passion. The Bible was suddenly filled with life and each week I read passages with a group of friends. I couldn't wait to attend these meetings. These readings laid the foundation for a dialectic that remains with me: drawing principles for living from the Bible, praying and talking them through with friends and then applying them in practical day-to-day situations. But there was a nagging uncertainty. Did this all add up? Or were these experiences merely an enthusiastic response that would fizzle out and die? I decided to extend my full-time studies and read theology for a year to see whether the claims of Christianity could stand up to the rigours of academic examination. During this time I learnt the grammar of the faith and found overwhelming evidence for the truth of Christ's claims to be God. Since then, I have never wobbled on the essential truth of the gospel story, although the implications have brought many questions and doubts. I also realized that theology was not merely a descriptive tool, useful in understanding the world better, but that the Christian task was to find God's way in the world and to work to change the world. I have been fired up by this challenge ever since.

Like many students leaving university, I felt overwhelmed by the prospect of choosing a career, as there were too many choices and too many questions about the purpose of work. I had read law and always assumed I would be a lawyer, yet increasingly I felt this might not be a good match for my personality, especially as I realized that I am not stimulated by detail. Having decided what not to do, the question of what to do remained. I knew that I could not work in South Africa, as I questioned the legitimacy of its government and I did not want to participate in an unjust economic system.

I needed an overall framework to answer the question of whether the pursuit of profit was selfish or a true contribution to society. I came to realize that the New Testament was vigorously opposed to selfishness but clearly distinguished the possessive individualism of self-centredness from self-interest. We are, after all, to love our neighbour as ourselves. I became convinced that democratic capitalism, despite its defects, was the economic system which served the common good and which best reflected the New Testament principles of justice, individual freedom and responsible risk-taking.

Of course, over the years I have had my doubts about the market economy. Sometimes it appears that the demand for efficiency unfairly discriminates against the weaker members of society. How can we justify the world becoming more efficient if it is more efficiently unfair? This particularly troubled me in recent times, when there seemed to be a headlong, compassionless pursuit of financial reward without restraint. These questions remain: but I have not found a better system. The market economy remains a good servant but a bad master – it needs to operate within a wider moral context which sees all human beings, and all the world's resources, as valuable, precisely because they matter to God. Without a values-based architecture, the market economy is weak in its foundations.

To be a Christian in the world today is therefore not comfortable. We will be challenged and left uneasy as we are constantly prodded by the Holy Spirit to question the ways in which the market economy serves the Christian objectives of justice and fairness. Our task is a distinctive one as we live our lives as witnesses of the Judaeo-Christian values which undergird so much of the market economy.

These were the sorts of questions I struggled with as I made my career choice. I had an interview with a theological college and realized that theological training was not the route for me. A bishop even offered me a job, but there was no peace in my heart. As I thought, prayed, chatted to people and visited the careers office, banking and insurance started to emerge as the most promising possibilities. I therefore spoke to two friends working in those areas who were both older Christians and recent graduates, and who believed in the importance of faith at work. I decided to apply for jobs in both fields. I was rejected by three banks and two insurance companies, leaving me with a choice between one insurance company and one small merchant bank in the City of London. I felt the responsibility of the choice before me not only as it affected me, but any wife and family I might have in the future. I knew that God had plans for my life and that he was a party to the decision and not merely an observer. I prayed each day for God's guidance, reciting this verse from Psalm 37:5: 'Commit your way to the Lord; trust in him, and he will do this.' I waited. There was no blinding light showing the path ahead but, instead, a growing conviction took hold of me that the banking door should be pushed first. I still felt sore about being rejected by the glamorous international banks, but nonetheless I accepted a London-based merchant banking job.

Merchant banks were the forerunners of investment banks: they are not high-street banks but financial institutions providing advisory, trading, and capital market services to sovereign governments and major financial institutions and corporations. Memorably I started work on the day of a sterling crisis, when the pound was plummeting against the US dollar, and the government and the Bank of England were trying to halt the slide. I thus caught my first sight of the gripping fear and uncertainty that can dominate financial markets. A bemused colleague commented that, as nothing practical could avert the crisis, my theological training qualified me better than any of the panicking dealers. 'You', he said, 'can at least pray.' So my career started.

Since then, I have prayed at work every day, almost without exception. I have tried to find time to pray at the start of the day, but often my prayers have been snatched between meetings or while travelling. I wish it weren't so, but the demands of the working day in an investment bank and of being married and having four children are not conducive to uninterrupted times of serene meditation. But these times, however imperfect, have equipped me for my work and reminded me daily of my reason for living and my dependence on God.

Living as a Christian in the world today is like living on a knife edge. Reading the Bible, praying and talking to friends are all helpful, but there is no 'click here' answer to the many dilemmas that we all face at work each day. A few years ago I went to the Namibian desert with a small group of Christian friends for a short break. For all of us, there was something very captivating about the arid vastness of the landscape, its stark desolation and its lack of distractions. In different ways each one of us wanted to hear from God. We prayed and worshipped together, and at sunset one evening, surrounded by silence and the unforgettable darkness of Africa, we had a communion service under the stars on the sand. Next morning, we got up before sunrise to walk along one of the largest and most majestic sand dunes in the world. What we saw was remarkable. As the sun rose, on one side there was pure light; on the other, a still and eerie darkness. As I was walking along the top of the dune I had the sense that this was a picture of the world in which Christians live. We were called to walk on the narrow ledge of the dune, not in darkness and not always in the sunlit beauty of the light side, but all the time leaning towards the light and away from the shadow.

The life of the Christian at work is a leaning towards goodness. Day by day we can sense God's presence as we avoid the darkness. We try to walk along this narrow divide, straining towards the light.

The workplace is a tough place but I have been encouraged by the belief that God has called us to be strengthened in the world for the world. This means embracing the challenges of a competitive world, and growing through them in order to help others to do the same. Knowing that we are placed in the world not by random accident but by God's design has carried me through many a difficult day.

During the last 30 years, being a Christian at work has, if anything, become more difficult. In part, this is a response to the general angst of the world around us, from which no Christian is immune. Financial markets have become volatile, decisions more complex and few choices are clear-cut. The harsh compromises that seem inevitable in the workplace have become more pressing as economic demands have grown.

The workplace is the coalface where faith is tested and sharpened by day-to-day encounters with the ambiguities and stresses of modern commerce. Our faith is tested when we recognize our weaknesses at work and we learn more about our hard and soft spots in our working relationships precisely because we cannot always choose the people with whom we work. We are tested and refined, and interact, testily or graciously, with colleagues or press our own self-ishness ahead of the common good, or forget gratitude and miss God completely in the day-to-day frenzy of work. Each one of us has been there.

Some think that faith makes us immune from making wrong choices. I wish that were so. God gives us the spiritual resources to grow through our weaknesses and to recover when we succumb to the ever-present temptations. The accusation of hypocrisy is the most hurtful. Others rightly expect those who embrace faith at work to act con-sistently with these values. We do not always do so. What I find hardest in others' judgement is that no allowance is made for the weakness that is common to all of us. But I have come to appreciate each day not only the fellowship of believers to help and to encourage but also the critical – and not always helpful – reactions of colleagues. Through a combination of these I believe we grow into the rounded, well-adjusted human beings that we are meant to be. None of us becomes a model of virtue instantly: life is lived out at work as part of a process, a learning experience. The greatest obstacle to maturing in our faith is ceasing to be teachable.

For the most part, I have had the privilege of hugely enjoying my work. In his book, *Joy at Work*, Dennis Bakke, the former co-founder and chief executive of one of the largest energy companies in the world, discusses the ways in which 'fun' became an essential core value of his company, in addition to the common principles of integrity, fairness and social responsibility. His Christian faith led him to the view that: 'Joy at work gives people the freedom to use their talents and skills for the benefit of society without being crushed or controlled by autocratic supervisors or staff officers.' Many work without this element of joy. One of the purposes of this book is to explore ways of recovering it.

But there are moments when a sense of depression seems to hover over me at work. The causes are often deep-seated, but the triggers go off unexpectedly – a failed transaction, a disappointing pay review, unpleasant relationships, fear of the future. These times of trial happen to everyone. They are, however, opportunities for God to be glorified. Paul said, 'When I am weak, then I am strong' (2 Corinthians 12:10). I have come to see that weakness is very hard to show in the workplace unless we remember its object is strength – our dependence on God.

No Christian truly comes of age until he or she grasps personally the truth of dying to the world. Paul, writing to the Galatians, says, 'I have been crucified with Christ and I no longer live, but Christ lives in me. The life I live in the body, I live by faith in the Son of God, who loved me and gave himself for me' (Galatians 2:20). For me, this rite of passage happened after a long period of restless debate about the purpose of life at work. In the early years, I was unclear that the work I was doing had any significance to God. I remember walking down the street that leads to the Bank of England one lunch time. I saw ahead of me the fortress-like Bank of England, and to my left, the sign to the Swiss Bank Corporation (where I would later work). I remember looking at these signs – they projected great security. But then, in a flash, I saw the truth. No bank – Swiss Bank or Bank of England – would survive the promised return of Christ. Strong as they appeared, their apparent security would be broken in an instant.

I also realized in that moment the illusory nature of the idea of 'job security'. True security can only be found in God's promises of security, both now and after death. I saw that Christ was in total control of all of life. Christ's death on the cross had broken the grip of this most forceful presence in my life. I knew that I had died with Christ and now lived a new life in him. I could walk free from compulsive greed, false financial security and captive illusions about the meaning of life. This did not mean that temptation ceased, nor that I never made wrong choices. But it did mean that the inevitability of being enthralled to the world was broken.

Can love flourish in the workplace? The idea is strained, not only because of the debased use of the word 'love' to describe mere sexual encounters but also because it is thought of as a 'soft virtue', not one of the hard values that make for successful organizations. Surely the competitive drive of the business world forces love off the agenda. But if love is central to the faith and if we are to be known by our love, how can it be excluded from the workplace? Love is the root motivation of service. Organizations frequently make the mistake of believing that good service to customers and clients can somehow be divorced from the internal attitudes of employees. But the opposite is the truth. When there are good internal attitudes, external service flourishes.

Dennis Bakke, in his book, puts it this way:

It is love that allows us to treat each person in our organisation with respect and dignity. Love sends people around the world to serve others. Love inspires people to work with greater purpose . . . love makes it possible for me to forgive those who derided my views and caused me so much pain. Because love is directed towards others, it allows for the possibility that my critics were right and I was wrong. And if I was wrong, I would hope that love would enable my detractors to forgive the forceful ways I have pushed my philosophy. I continue to believe that love is the final crucial ingredient in a joy-filled workplace . . . love is perfectly consistent with even the most aggressive economic goals.

Love remains for me the key inheritance of faith and the missing jewel of happiness in the modern workplace. I hope this book will in a small way also help to recover the value and power of love at work.

My current role involves being responsible for building relationships with key clients. I advise them on their strategies, help them to buy and sell companies and sometimes defend them from unwanted predators. I recognize that my experience may be different from yours. However, in conversation over the years with people working in very different jobs from mine, I have come to see that the underlying issues are similar for all Christians. Many people, at all stages of their working lives, have asked me questions about work and spirituality. I have been especially challenged by the questions of those in their twenties who are embarking on their careers, and those who are experiencing doubts about their role in the workplace. I have put pen to paper, I confess reluctantly, as I do not find it easy to speak about myself. I can only hope that from my own experience of hardship and joy in the workplace, you may catch some glimpse of God at work, and that he may help you as he has helped me. This book is for those who are already engaged in the exciting challenge of living out their Christian faith at work. It is also for those exploring the bigger questions of life who would describe themselves as sympathetic to Christianity, but not quite as shareholders.

Work Matters

Many Christians do not see God as a 24/7 Creator. Instead, he has become a withdrawn actor confined to a Sunday show with a declining audience. A working faith is often seen as a contradictory notion. For many it is as quaint to have a working faith as to have a working mill: it is of passing antiquarian interest but hardly useful in a modern economy. Yet the world of work belongs not in the slipstream of twenty-first century Christian spirituality, but in its mainstream. That's how God meant it to be. We will only take our faith to work if we know that our work is valuable to God.

God at work

Our paradigms for work are found both in God's initiatives in creation and in our understanding of the Trinity. As God laboured in creation, so he expects us to do the same. Indeed, creation and work were interlinked as God gave us a mandate to act as stewards of the created order, establishing a community on earth based on mutual service. It is deep in God's character to work because it is deep in God's character to serve. The God of the Bible is not a passive, detached spiritual being but a dynamic, active and entrepreneurial being. Work was God's idea in the first place and therefore matters to him. He wanted to share on earth what he saw working to perfection in the heavenly community of Father, Son and Holy Spirit. God had the desire to create for us on earth the same attributes of sharing, service, partnership and collaboration that are enjoyed in the Godhead. We are made in God's image: we are, in one sense, chips off the old block. The mutual dependence of the members of the Trinity – the Father needing the Son, the Son obeying the Father and the Spirit linking them together in love – is a picture of unity, co-operation and, at the same time, respect for each person's different functions.

God worked with extraordinary energy in creation, to make the world, the animals and, supremely, human life. He worked at full tilt to a timeline. In Genesis Chapter 1, we read of his creative activities in making the heaven and the earth. After each day's work he had the supreme reward, implanted in all entrepreneurs, of reviewing each stage of his work, and seeing that it was good (Genesis 1:4). Moreover, life was created not as a one-off specification. He blessed the living creatures and commanded them to grow and to supply the earth and waters with increased production (Genesis 1:22). Above all, he created people with a delegated authority of care and maintenance and a specific brief to cultivate the Garden of Eden, to 'work it and take care of it' (Genesis 2:15). Although he felt good at each stage of the job he did not stop until the task was completed satisfactorily (Genesis 2). Then he took time out and 'rested from all the work of creating that he had done' (Genesis 2:3). He had worked with a purpose to establish a right order in creation.

Adam and Eve experienced fulfilment as human beings as they served God in their work, which was as closely allied to God's purposes as it was possible to be. Enjoyment, freedom and happiness at work reflected the virtues ingrained in the Godhead, in whose image humanity was made. Then Adam and Eve were drawn away from God, and they had to make the harsh adjustment to encumbered work. Futility, despair, recrimination, broken relationships and ultimately death entered the world and the workplace. Work became a curse (Genesis 3:17–19). The whole created order broke away from its co-operation with God. The ground was cursed, work became 'painful' and never-ending – a living had to be earned by the sweat of our brows.

But everything within the Creator wanted to restore work to its original specification. A new initiative was needed to enable the broken model to work again. Jesus was sent to repair the fractured working relationship between us and God. He came to pay off the debt that bound work to futility.

Work – fulfilment or futility?

Work now exists in a tension between fulfilment and futility. On the one hand we know the presence of God at work, creating, innovating and filling us with energy. We see signs of his activity in the many ways in which we flourish at work and feel good about our achievements. On the other hand we know the futility of work, the lack of direction, the struggle to get things done, the fear of the future, the lack of purpose and direction. How then should we live at work? At its best our work is an example of a close partnership between us and God as we draw his values into the working world, making the most of what God has given us and not oscillating between a purpose-led life and futility. We live and work in the power of the Resurrection, through which death, the ultimate futility, has been defeated. Christian work – best understood as service – survives death. As we work on earth, so we will in eternity. Work pre-dates the Fall. It was part of God's original plan for humanity. God will therefore maintain the best of the original creation when He calls into being the new creation.

To make the most of our lives we need to have a clear view of God's intentions for us in the workplace: to serve him and our community and to enjoy a measure of success, to grow in our humanity and to influence the world for good as we wait for Jesus to return. This is not merely a case of chalking up air miles while we are alive to be spent in heaven after death. Eternal life starts here as we live well for God, reflecting his original intentions by participating in turning round the broken image of work.

Working together

Paul uses the metaphor of the body to describe the Christian community. The project team at work is no different. As each part of the body performs a vital function, so each member of a team is similarly invaluable. The finance person on the project is as important in achieving a good result as the marketing person. In working towards a successful conclusion, the project leader is hamstrung without the input of the junior executive. Finding a way of recognizing different functions, respecting differences and yet being bound together to produce a result is an enriching experience precisely because it reflects the God-given roots of our creation.

Work will never be perfected until the return of Jesus, but until then it is possible, through the power of his Spirit, to live and work together with purpose, direction and enjoyment, even though, for now, these have to be enjoyed imperfectly.

My work station is my worship station

A new trainee once told me, as we were discussing the purpose of work:

> Let's face it. We work to make money, to live and to enjoy ourselves. It makes life bearable even if work sucks. What's so wrong with that?

So why do we work? There are many biblical reasons for working: economic – to create wealth; financial – to support oneself and a family; personal – to experience fulfilment and significance; social – to avoid being a burden on others; relational – to support other people through collaborative effort. God is interested in the good of the whole of society. So when I am asked about worship I reply firmly, 'My work station is my worship station.' Worship is the total submission of our whole person to the glory of God as we recognize our dependence on him. My desk should therefore be a place of worship. Indeed, the Hebrew word for work and worship is the same – *avodah*. God is our real employer. In his letter to the Colossians, Paul urges us: 'Whatever you do, work at it with all your heart, as working for the Lord, not for human masters' (Colossians 3:23). I remember a personal assistant telling me that when she passed the reception desk on her way into work each morning, she reminded herself, 'It is the Lord Christ I serve.' This avoids the danger of settling for satisfactory underperformance. I try to pray every morning as I start work because I want to remind myself that I am not dependent on myself or on any economic system, but on God. Work is a ministry, empowered by God, for the benefit of ourselves and others, and ultimately for his glory.

I love reading the Bible through the lens of someone at work. There are so many characters from whom we can learn: ordinary people with ordinary jobs. Paul, for example, was in the manufacturing industry as a tentmaker and clearly expected others to work. When he wrote to the Thessalonians, he said, '. . . work with your hands, just as we told you, so that your daily life may win the respect of outsiders and so that you will not be dependent on anybody' (1 Thessalonians 4:11b–12). Abraham was a wealthy cattle trader; Joseph worked as Prime Minister, but also dealt in wheat futures; Luke was a doctor; the first Ethiopian convert was a central banker; Dorcas was in fashion; Lydia was a businesswoman; Cornelius, an army general; Simon the tanner was the Louis Vuitton of his times; Jesus himself grew up learning the trade of carpentry.

As a young man, Jesus, like many of his contemporaries,

would probably have worked in the family business with Joseph, learning skills both in manufacturing and in dealing with people. We can easily imagine Jesus purchasing wood and nails, making a window or door, negotiating a price and selling his work. In these hidden years, Jesus must have come into contact with a cross-section of the community in Nazareth. This is reflected in his teaching, which includes workers in the vineyard, meetings with tax collectors, dealings with agents and discussions about money, livestock and property. We know that he aligned himself totally with his Father's work: 'My Father is always at his work to this very day, and I, too, am working' (John 5:17). He did not come to give us a new form of spiritual life disconnected from the world. He came to continue and restore the patterns of work and service initiated by his Father.

And now, through his Spirit, we are reminded that work was in the original God-breathed prospectus of service.

Holy jobs – bishops and bankers

William Tyndale, the translator of the Bible into English, in *A Parable of the Wicked Mammon*, said that:

> There is no work better than another to please God;
> to pour water, to wash dishes, to be a souter
> [cobbler], or an apostle, all is one; to wash dishes

and to preach is all one, as touching the deed, to
please God.

We need not only to recover this understanding, but also
to rid ourselves of the view that there is a religious pecking
order in God's sight where bishops rank ahead of bankers
and ordained clergy ahead of computer programmers. Few
distinctions can have been so disastrous in the history of
the church as that between the sacred, i.e. the ordained
ministry, and the secular, i.e. other callings. This distinction is deep rooted, going back to the medieval exaltation
of the clergy, and continuing to the time when the links
between God and ordinary daily life were severed in the
name of progress and reason. Clericalism had left the edu-
cated clerical class as the sole exponents of Christianity,
disenfranchising everyone else. But Paul draws no distinction between hard spiritual work and hard work in the
workplace. He uses the same words for manual labour as
for his apostolic service. For me, this realization transformed the way in which I viewed the workplace. God was
interested in every aspect of my life. At church on Sunday,
we may pray for the leaders of the church and society, but
how often do we pray for Jill the accountant and Mark the
salesman in the third row?

Christians have, at times, adopted the great fallacy that
an emigration from the world of work would produce a

spirituality of a higher order, which would therefore be more pleasing to God. The monastic tradition, often blamed for this withdrawal from the world, has, on the contrary, a high view of work. We cannot, and were never intended by God the Creator to, take exit visas from the world to escape its pressures. Dietrich Bonhoeffer, in *Letters and Papers from Prison*, spoke of the calling of Christians to be 'this worldly', living amongst the harsh realities of life and demonstrating our faith by the day-to-day choices we make. Before Jesus is arrested, he prays for his disciples: 'My prayer is not that you take them out of the world but that you protect them from the evil one' (John 17:15).

The false division of the sacred and the secular struck me particularly in the flawed London Millennium Dome, which was constructed at enormous cost as a national centre to commemorate the millennium. In the Dome, life was divided into various spheres of activity including a spirit zone, a transaction zone and a work zone. The clear message was that the spirit zone was very different from any other part of our lives. This distinction is as big a disaster for fulfilled Christian living as indeed the Dome was nationally. One cannot say that church is a 'God zone' while the workplace is a 'God-free zone'. Christianity involves our whole lives. We therefore need to live according to our Christian values in every area of our lives. I find it hugely challenging to ask myself each day how my own values have been influenced by the world and the degree to which they have shifted away from God towards myself.

In the *Christian Herald*, Mark Cazalid said:

> When I commit myself and my work into God's hands it means there is no split between the sacred and the secular, so everything I do becomes interconnected and part of my dialogue with God.

The principal casualty of the world's pathological turning away from God is the destruction of our humanity. This God-given humanity has to be fulfilled in the workplace if we are to be true to the good news of Jesus reaching every part of our lives. A key executive in a London trading firm told me that his life at work had been completely transformed when he began to understand that God loved him as much in the frenzied atmosphere of the dealing room as at home or at church. In Colossians Paul says, 'He is before all things, and in him all things hold together' (Colossians 1:17). Of all aspects of Christianity in the modern world, this is the one that excites me most: the creative energy of God is at work each day, gripping and knitting together every part of our lives.

Computers and capital – what's the point?

> I've never been able to see how this computer has
> anything to do with the kingdom of God.
>
> (Jim Banks, computer programmer)

When Jesus came to earth, he proclaimed that the kingdom of God was at hand. The language of kingdoms can sound strange to us, in that it seems to signify territoriality. In the context of work, it may therefore be helpful to see the kingdom of God as 'the sphere of God's goodness' in the world. We are called to advance that kingdom, sharing the 'sphere of goodness' and extending it as we operate with God's values. Our actions at work have the potential to advance the kingdom of God and his 'sphere of goodness', or to hinder it – on both a macro and a micro level.

We need to grasp this truth with vigour if we are to be convinced that the workplace is where God wants us to be. I am often asked the question whether it would not be better to work for a charity or for a church than in the business world. I understand the question but the answer is not obvious and relies on the mistaken belief that God is more interested in the apparently greater humanitarian activities of a charity than he is in normal work. He isn't. He wants us to know how much he values our workplaces, so that we are free to work without guilt. Some, of course, will be called to work in the voluntary sector. Most of us will find our callings in the secular workplace and will need to find out how to be fulfilled there. In practice, it is easier to see this in some jobs, such as nursing or social work, than in others.

How then does working as a banker in a large organization advance the kingdom of God? An executive, who had worked in a bank for five years, told me, 'I feel so confused, I work in a big global institution but I am such a small and insignificant part of it that I can make no difference. What am I trying to achieve with my life?' (Dana Olsen, graduate trainee). I tried to help her understand the bigger picture. This is an essential requirement if we are to find the purpose behind our work.

The free flow of capital, the provision of funds for new business and the creation of jobs are all important to society. All of us need to understand the wider context of the jobs we do. The supermarket manager delivers a crucial service by providing good food at affordable prices. Effective management and customer service impacts the community by making shopping a positive experience. On the micro level, as we learn to see what God is doing in our workplaces we can then put our energies into those areas. For example, whether we describe a product accurately or not is a spiritual decision.

Somebody asks a shop assistant, 'Will the colour in this

jumper run if I put it in the washing machine?' When we declare truth even in small measures, the kingdom of God is advanced. This can be true when we draft documents, sell products, or mark exams – indeed, in any activity we do in our working day. We need to remind ourselves continuously that God is interested in building up his original plan of community. We often miss out this crucial reason for work by narrowing the discussion on the purpose of work to an individualistic debate about self-fulfilment. Instead this debate should be held in the context of the needs of the wider human community which God created, loves and which needs to be served by, for example, banks, supermarkets, and information technology.

Fruitful and faithful – how do we make a difference?

Most people want to make a difference with their lives. To do this, we have to identify our part in extending God's kingdom. The great task of the Christian in the world today is to bring blessing to the world. We are agents for good living in the world. We need therefore to be both fruitful and faithful in pursuing our God-given ambitions.

In the parable of the talents (Luke 19:11–27), the master, before going on a journey to have himself appointed king, gives his servants some capital and urges them to put it to work until he returns. When he returns, he rewards the two servants who have put the money to good use and have made more from the initial gift, associating themselves with him in his absence, despite his general lack of popularity. However, he is angry with the servant who merely preserved the initial capital without taking the necessary risks to make it grow.

We need to be faithful to God, willing to associate ourselves with his values in the workplace. This may risk our reputations, because as Christians, we have to face the taunt that there is no God. And if there is one, as in the parable, he appears to have gone on a long holiday. We, however, behave each day in the knowledge that Jesus will return and reward us as well as call us to account.

I remember being on holiday in the south of France and seeing a magnificent yacht moored in harbour. She had a crew of 24. I met the captain, who was having coffee in the harbour. I asked him about the yacht. He told me that every day the crew took her out to sea to check on safety procedures. Every day the yacht was cleaned to perfection. She was provisioned, and every day they were ready to sail. He then added wistfully, 'We have not seen or heard from the owner for nearly three years, but we are ready to set sail the moment he arrives, and I know he will turn up one day, I hope soon.' This is how we should live, getting on with the job in hand as we anticipate the return of Jesus.

We are to be fruitful as well as faithful. We need growth in all areas of life – there is no steady state. Our talents, money, time and resources are all God's gift to us and should be used well. Making the most of them will involve risk. The key point of this parable is that the hand of fruitfulness needs the glove of faithfulness in order to grasp the opportunities that we are given. We cannot merely be faithful, simply taking what God has given us, preserving it, pickling it and then producing it upon his return. Equally, we cannot merely be fruitful, simply adding to the resources he has given, without recognizing at the same time that we are servants awaiting the return of our master. This message is summarized by Paul when he urges us to 'make the most of every opportunity' (Colossians 4:5).

The world – to comfort or confront?

God loves the world. This is evident throughout Scripture and given full expression in John 3:16: 'For God so loved the world that he gave his one and only Son, that whoever believes in him shall not perish but have eternal life.' Yet John also warns us: 'Do not love the world or anything in the world' (1 John 2:15). The apparent contradiction in these verses is easily resolved. We are not to 'love the world', meaning that part of creation which seeks to run itself without any reference to God. This world view is articulated, for example, through the media, which often reflects opinions made by people for people, but without the acknowledgement of God. The theologian Walter Bruggeman calls this absence of God 'the defining pathology of our time'. The world in this wrong-headed sense cannot recognize the hand of God; and because it is on a trajectory to destruction, we are not to set our hearts on it. However, we are to love the world that God has created: the environment (which he has given to us to preserve for future generations) and the people, whom God created and for whom Christ died.

Our workplaces are structured organizations. In the course of a career many of us will both be managed and manage others and most of us will have peer colleagues. These distinctions affect both the information that it is appropriate to share and our method of communication. However, we need to remember that people are still people. Behind the suits live vulnerable people in need of affirmation and support. All of us need commendation and recognition for the positive things we do at work. Day to day we need to seek opportunities to go against the grain: to offer small acts of kindness or words of encouragement to our colleagues, or simply to be positive in negative situations. I know a lawyer who makes a point of complimenting at least one person in the office each day. His aim is to counter the negative words spoken around him.

Learning to love our neighbour, surely the hallmark of the Christian faith, is tested each day in the fire of the workplace.

In John 17, Jesus outlines this inherent tension, saying that his followers are in the world but not of the world. By this, he means that although we aim to operate by the values of the kingdom of God, geographically we are located in the workplaces of the world. As we walk through the fields of life, we pick up burrs of loneliness, disappointment and purposelessness. We find ourselves both bearing and breaking the image of a dysfunctional society. This is the daily confrontation in the workplace and this tension leads to a constant negotiation of complex issues for which there are no pre-agreed outcomes. In one sense, the workplace is a battleground, but the victory is assured. I constantly remind myself that 'no weapon that is formed against [me] shall prosper' (Isaiah 54:17, KJV). We still have to live with uncertainty and complexity but we have not been left without assistance; the Holy Spirit comes alongside to help us.

How then do we make the most of living in the world? Many Christians have a way of looking at the world with an ingrained pessimism. Preachers, wishing to draw distinctions, can also fall into this habit of describing the world in lurid terms in order to accentuate the theme of the great escape to salvation. The willingness to criticize the world and its aspirations at every opportunity has caused an imbalance in our attitude to the world. How do we correct this perspective while remaining alive to the seductive nature of the world and its aspirations? I have found three approaches to be helpful.

1. Understanding the world

Jesus wanted people to understand reality. We need to learn from him and to sharpen our analytical tools when trying to understand the world before we launch into a critical tirade against its defects. Our first rule of engagement with the world is therefore to try to *understand* its aspirations and desires and to embrace its goodness. I was struck by reading the parable of the unjust steward in Luke 16:1–8, where Jesus makes what appears to be a cryptic conclusion. He says that the 'people of this world' are often shrewder in dealing with the issues facing them in the world than the people of light (meaning those of faith). Jesus seems to be suggesting that the world understands itself better than outsiders do. When we listen to contemporary music, watch films, or study advertising messages, we soon discover this to be true.

During one of our annual church conferences I led a seminar entitled, 'How to do life'. The objective of the seminar was to examine whether the world was an enlightened or a dark place. This is a crucial question for anyone trying to live for Christ in the workplace. We need a biblical world view if we are to live meaningful lives in the world. At the seminar I reviewed with the group the advertising of Coca Cola over the last 20 years. The desire for purpose, love, community, family, and motivation was matched by the slogans, 'Coke is it' and 'You can't beat the real thing'; another was illustrated by two adjoining Coke bottles joined with the word 'Love'; 'All of us are friends of friends' showed many different people joining hands in a demonstration of community. These slogans were created as one of the world's leading corporations tried to understand and connect with the perceived needs of people. We thus learn from the media, song writers, advertisers and opinion-formers about the needs of the world.

Our understanding is improved when we become involved in discussion and dialogue with those who do not share Christian assumptions of life. By understanding where they are we can begin to help to shift the basis of their world view away from the fruitless search for meaning 'chasing after the wind' (Ecclesiastes 1:14), or the deficient solutions offered by the world.

2. Critiquing the world

It is, however, not sufficient merely to understand and to show empathy towards the world around us. Nor should we be gullible and allow the world to define its own solutions. There is a need for a rational and critical review of the defects of the world in which we live. The prevailing values of the world should be held to account to test whether these values are serving the interests of society or destroying them. So, for example, we assess the driving forces behind consumerism to determine how they are at odds with the biblical values of restraint and generosity to others. The world cannot produce solutions for unhappiness or lack of fulfilment at work, for fractured relationships or depression and stress – it has no answer for the world's conundrums: how, for example, to marry the desire for instant gratification with the long-term formation of character. A biblical critique is part of the process of establishing the vacuum that exists in the world's perceptions.

3. Drawing the world to Christ

After understanding the world and critiquing its failures, the third and distinctive engagement takes place. We are to be witnesses to the power of God's activity in reconciling the world to himself. The way ahead lies not merely in understanding the wider needs of our colleagues more clearly, nor in the skill with which these needs are examined and commented upon. Real change comes from being able to introduce Christ's teaching and power into the dialogue with the world. I do not see this in adversarial terms but as part of a dialectic that starts with understanding, before it becomes prescriptive. Many have tried to seek reconciliation with the world by ducking the central Christian event – the cross – hoping to find the power to live in a cross-less spiritual experience. Such a route is doomed to fail. It is through the cross and resurrection that reconciliation with the world takes place. There are no short cuts and our challenge is to present this insight in everyday language to a world searching for its anchor.

Let us apply these three critical tools – understanding the world, critiquing the world and drawing the world to Christ – to the current debate on the search for happiness. While the pursuit of happiness is not a modern invention, there seems to be a new intensity about the contemporary quest for happiness. The leader of the Conservative party, David Cameron, urged us to remember 'what makes people happy, as well as what makes stock markets rise . . . it is time to be focused not just on GDP but on GWB – General Well Being.' The BBC tapped into this desire with a six part series, *The Happiness Formula*. A leading article in *The Sunday Times* described this search as follows:

It has become the great obsession, spawning dozens of books and growing a number of university and school courses here and in America. Happiness is in vogue . . .

What was previously left to philosophers is now the object of study by economists, social scientists and business schools. The John Lewis Partnership, one of the UK's most successful retailers, states unambiguously that 'the Partnership's ultimate purpose is the happiness of all its members through their worthwhile and satisfying employment in a successful business.' Happiness is important to all of us, whether viewed from a faith base or not. The Dalai Lama's book, *The Art of Happiness: A Handbook for Living*, is an international bestseller. William James, the American philosopher, spoke of happiness as the real motivation of all people: 'How to gain, how to keep, how to recover happiness, is in fact for most men at all times the secret motive of all they do, and of all they are willing to endure' (William James, *The Varieties of Religious Experience*).

The questions, however, leap out at once. Why do we have so much and are still unhappy? What is happiness? Where does it come from? Can it be taken in tablet form? Do we merely resign ourselves to Kant's comment, 'the concept of happiness is such an indeterminate one that even though everyone wishes to attain happiness, yet he can never say definitely and consistently what it is that he really wishes and wills' (*Grounding for the Metaphysics of Morals*)?

We understand the world's longing for happiness but also see the deficiency of its tools in trying to understand the nature of true happiness. But even in terms of prevailing values without a distinctively Christian interpretation, there is a recognition that this longing to be happy at work and in life generally is important and not merely a current fad.

Happiness will not be found in mere possessions, more spending, greater material prosperity or greater job satisfaction. Happiness and purposeful living go together. When asked what it was like to be the wealthiest person in the world, Bill Gates replied that he wished he was not the richest man. But I don't know anyone who would not want to be the happiest person in the world. On a smaller scale we need to ask the question of whether our daily working lives are so focused on earning and advancement that we have neglected to find the source of sustainable happiness.

When we draw these desires together we realize that merely being happy for a day because a project has been successfully completed is not enough. To be truly happy requires something greater than the satisfaction of my own interests. Helping others, being generous with time as well as with money, and being prepared to put the interests of others before those of one's self show the altruism inherent in the search for happiness.

What then does Christian spirituality have to offer a generation longing for consistent day-in and day-out happiness in the workplace? Here we hit the reality block. Christian values, based on the teachings of Jesus, are often counter cultural. It is simply not possible to live in a cocooned world expecting to be happy every moment. To believe this would be to live in an unreal fool's paradise. Jesus says that in this world we will have tribulation. But, as ever, while recognizing the reality of living in a world adrift from its Creator's moorings, Jesus goes on to promise: 'But take heart! I have overcome the world' (John 16:33). There will therefore be times of sorrow, mourning, hard times and unhappiness. There will also be days when, if we are honest, we feel neither one way nor the other and life goes on. What we need to do, therefore, is to enter a dialogue of reality with those searching for happiness and base this interchange upon the teachings of Christ. Happiness is therefore re-defined not just as an unlinked series of fleeting feelings of enjoyment but as a part of the overall search for purpose in life. The closer we live in line with the wisdom of Christ's teachings the more we will be able to accept the joy of moments of happiness while also being able to live with the down times. The truth is that our search for happiness will be most fulfilled when seen through the lens of Christ's teaching on sacrifice, service, contentment and joy. When we allow the interests of others to flourish at work at our expense we may well feel tugs of unhappiness, but in the overall scheme of living for Christ these acts of self-denial become a pattern of lasting joy, which St Paul sums up when he says: 'For me to live is Christ' (Philippians 1:21). True joy, happiness and fulfilment run together when the focus moves from ourselves on to helping to satisfy the needs and aspirations of others. So the Living Bible translation rightly paraphrases the 'Blessed are those' sayings in the Sermon on the Mount as 'Happy are those . . .' 'Happy are those who long to be just and good for they shall be completely satisfied' (Matthew 5:6). They may know times of unhappiness but they are happy overall because they have been satisfied by knowing that they are living by the original plan of God's intentions to all people on earth.

In this way, we understand the world's longing for happiness, recognize that even by its own standards happiness will not be obtained through the pursuit of materialist solutions, and point to the cross and resurrection to reinterpret happiness: when understood in this light, this makes sense of the pursuit of happiness.

An image that I find helpful is that of the television

screen. If you turn on a news channel or business channel, not only do you see the images of current world events unfolding, but below the pictures there is often a running text giving additional information. I see this as an illustration of the Christian's interaction with the world. As we see and hear world events breaking we should constantly be running a biblical commentary on these events, interpreting actions and reminding ourselves that we only truly come to understand the world in and through Christ.

Too often, the church has tried to urge people to live by the values of Christ without paying sufficient attention to the pressures of day-to-day life, appearing self-righteous in its judgements as well as being insensitive and escapist. As we engage with society's issues, we are called to confront anything that draws people away from God, but at the same time to comfort those who are struggling. But how often does our society end up confronting those who need comforting and comforting those who need confronting?

Sometimes the harsh working environment seems the last place I would expect to meet God. However, Jesus experienced the worst of the world on the cross. My office may seem very far from the goodness of God; but in fact, he has gone a lot further. The cross is the furthest place of human despair. He went there for us. However godless an office may appear, it is not beyond his reach. It is not a no-God area. Jesus' resurrection is the constant reminder of life beyond the struggle. In hard times, when the world seems to close in on us or we become self-obsessed, I have found that repeating aloud the simple truth that 'Christ is risen' has a transforming power. This is the pointer to life in all its fullness. The reminder that tomorrow will come is the assurance we all need to enable us to live in hope each day. This knowledge provides daily reassurance as we face a tough workplace.

People matter to God and therefore to us. An important aspect of loving those we work with is to pray for them, mostly without them knowing. We may be aware that there are people in our workplace with questions about the meaning of life and the existence of God, who would value our input as part of their search. We need to be ready to answer when asked about our faith, clearly and without embarrassment. Our prime task at work is not to be evangelists. That is not what we are employed to do. But we should be vigilant and available to colleagues at decisive moments when we can discuss with them the way towards a spirituality that will enrich their lives.

The thoughts of this chapter can best be summed up in the story of a friend of mine:

I was brought up in a Christian family in New Zealand, with my great grandfather being a Methodist missionary. When I was ten years old my

younger sister died and my parents were divorced
soon after. Our family then drifted away from our
faith. When I graduated, I chose a career in banking,
and found myself working at Warburg's in London in
the early 1990s. I was achieving the career and financial objectives I'd set myself; I'd married a beautiful
American woman; we spent our weekends in roman-
tic European cities – what more could I want? I
found myself feeling strangely empty, but resolutely
dismissed the emotion as 'Sunday night blues'. But
increasingly I wondered, 'Is there more to life than
this?'

I was working for a man called Ken Costa, and
found myself regularly travelling in taxis with him to
and from meetings. The traffic in London is terrible,
so there was a lot of time to talk! Ken found out
somehow about the scrap of Christianity in my life,
and invited me to an Alpha Supper. When my wife,
Katie, questioned me on the invitation, I told her
that the guy was my boss and we had to go! The
truth was, though, that I had come to respect him,
and was curious about his views. We duly turned up
and Nicky Gumbel gave a talk. The talk was excellent
but what interested me were the people who stood
up and said that God was filling an emptiness inside
them, the very emotion with which I wrestled.

To be honest, Ken played no further part in my search for God. He never mentioned Alpha again. He had effectively stepped aside to let God do the work. At the Alpha Weekend I became a Christian, and subsequently engineered lunch with Ken to ask him a burning question: Must I give all this up and become a missionary to India? I dreaded the answer. But Ken assured me that God does not lead us out of jobs, but into them, and I stayed in investment banking.

Soon after, Katie and I moved to Australia, and became involved in Alpha at our local church in Melbourne. In 1998, whilst still working full-time in investment banking, I became Chairman of Alpha Australia. In 2000, I joined the board of Alpha International. At the beginning of 2004, walking along a beach in Sydney, Nicky Gumbel asked me to become Chairman of Alpha Asia Pacific. Finally, I was called out of investment banking as God gave me a passion to fulfil this new role. It is a huge challenge to work in this vast region, containing two-thirds of the world's population. I am using all the skills honed over 20 years in banking, but now of course I am doing deals for God!

In 1991, I was terrified of becoming a missionary to India. In March 2005, in a meeting in Mumbai, I suddenly realized I *had* become a missionary to

India. And now I find myself sitting on the Alpha International Board with Ken Costa, and even occasionally sharing a taxi!

Ambition and Life Choices

The word 'ambition' elicits a mixed response. For Johnny Depp, 'Ambition has become a dirty word.' So too Radiohead: 'Ambition makes you look pretty ugly.' But it's not all negative. When we speak of an athlete who wants to win a gold medal, we applaud their single-minded ambition.

Many Christians regard ambition for anything other than 'saving souls' as a distraction from our true calling to evangelism. This is a misunderstanding of the Bible: God has called us to extend his kingdom in the world in partnership with him. It is surely right to be ambitious about our contribution to this. In 1 Chronicles 4:10, Jabez prayed that God would bless him and increase his possessions. Christians sometimes feel that it is inappropriate to pray for opportunity and success at work. Yet Jabez is described as 'more honourable than his brothers' (1 Chronicles 4:9). If our ambition is aligned with what God has called us to do, then we are right to ask for his blessing on it so that we can make a difference in the world and bring him glory.

Sir Rocco Forte, who lost a hotel chain built up by his father and went on to build a chain of his own, sums up the desires of many when he reflects: 'I don't want to go through life and for people to say "What have you done?" and to say "Nothing". I like to feel that I've made an impact, left something behind.'

Passionate and contented – what is Christian ambition?

For me, Christian ambition is the passionate and contented pursuit of challenging yet attainable God-given objectives.

Passionate

Roy Hattersley, in his biography of General Booth, *Blood and Fire*, describes the 'reckless enthusiasm' that led Booth to form the Salvation Army. Similarly, our ambitions should arise from a God-given passion: to fulfil his purpose for our lives. In Philippians, Paul writes, 'It is God who works in you *to will* and to act according to his good purpose' (Philippians 2:13, italics mine).

Jean-Pierre Garnier, the head of GlaxoSmithKline, one of the world's largest pharmaceutical companies, puts it succinctly: 'I don't know anyone who is passionate and unsuccessful'.

Contented

God gives us objectives that match our talents. If you are unsure of these, it may be worth using one of the many analytical tools available, such as *What Color Is Your Parachute?* by Richard Bolles, or the Gallup Strengths Finder, and to talk to those who know you well. The better we know ourselves, the more we can imagine what kind of work God might be calling us to. The close link between calling and gifting helps us to be contented as we do work that suits us. Contentedness is not particular to our personality type but comes from the knowledge that we are working for God in what he has called us to do. In our ambition to fulfil God-given goals, we can rely on his strength.

Challenging

My former vicar, John Collins, once told me, 'Do not settle for black and white if God has given you a vision in colour.' We should not worry if we feel daunted – God-inspired dreams should be challenging. Initially I was attracted by the money, travel and excitement of banking. Alongside that I became increasingly excited about seeing the kingdom of God grow in a secular society. This vision to see God at the heart of London life has developed and continues to inspire all aspects of my life.

Sir Terry Leahy, the head of Tesco, who is widely credited with having built up the Tesco business to its present commanding position, has defined this challenge as follows:

> . . . the essence of leadership is painting a vision that others will follow. Find out the truth of the situation, paint a picture of where you want to get to, make a plan and go and do it. It applies to businesses and cities *but it also applies to your own personal situation.* Always believe that there is a better place and then persuade people to get there *with you.*

Attainable

Our ambitions should stretch us but they should be achievable. I remember the original advertising campaign for Avis, the car rental company. Avis decided that their mission statement would be: 'We will be the second largest motor rental company in the world.' They knew that Hertz was unassailable as number one. With the slogan, 'We try harder', they recognized that they could grow their market share to the point where they could challenge Hertz. They were way down the pecking order so this was a tall but attainable order. We may not achieve all our ambitions, but they should be realistic. 'One day, when I am a billionaire, I shall be able to feed millions of people' is a worthy sentiment, but is not what

I mean by Christian ambition. It is challenging, but is it attainable?

God-given

Who can forget Eric Liddle's remark in *Chariots of Fire*: 'God made me for a purpose. He made me for China, but he also made me fast and when I run, I feel his pleasure' (1924 Olympics)? But perhaps the most frequent response we feel when we believe we are being drawn into a new venture is, 'Is this really you God?' It is a good question to ask. We need to know that our ambitions are initiated, sustained and, where necessary, corrected by God as we step out in faith to do his will.

Marketing or management – how do we make career choices?

Relationship

Much has been written on the subject of guidance. I have struggled myself to know God's specific will for my life and have talked at length to many at all stages of their working lives as they too grapple with the subject. Some of the following practical observations are distilled from these conversations.

As Christians our main reference point when making decisions is our relationship with God, developed through regular prayer and reading the Bible. A formative verse for me has been Psalm 25:14: 'The Lord confides in those who fear him; he makes his covenant known to them.'

It is an arresting thought that the Lord of all the world would choose to confide in us. Asking for guidance is therefore not wimping out of responsibility, or passively accepting the future, but an interactive process. This process deepens our faith. As we bring the impulses of our hearts and our creative ideas to God, we are often given wide choices. However, the language some use when speaking about guidance sometimes seems to imply that we are robots responding to the unchangeable direction of the programmer. I am often sceptical of the introductory phrase, 'God told me to leave my job.' If this is shorthand for a more interactive process, that is wonderful, but it sometimes indicates a misunderstanding of guidance, or worse a passing of the buck. It is only by accepting responsibility for our actions before God that we mature as human beings.

In many discussions with people leaving university or college and trying to choose from a number of career options, I have found a recurring malaise: paralysis. This paralysis comes from the constant plea for guidance in the expectation that God will make our decisions for us. In some ways it is like trying to enter the door of a vicarage. The vicar says, 'After you.' In politeness the visitor replies, 'After you.' 'No, no,' replies the vicar, 'after you.' 'Please,

please,' says the visitor, 'after you.' And so it goes on. Guidance can become a revolving door, ever turning, God expecting us to act and we expecting God to act. However, it is as we move forward and take the first step that we sense God's voice behind us saying, 'This is the way; walk in it' (Isaiah 30:21). I have no doubt that God expects us to be the first mover. This was well captured for me in a letter from a financier trying to make a critical decision:

> It usually helps to get a bit of motion before I can see where I am going. In a boat, it is difficult to navigate while you are still in the dock, but once out of the harbour, you can feel the currents and the wind and set a course.
>
> (Tosin Aderemi, banker)

I have found it helpful to talk to trusted friends when making big decisions. Some years ago I was sitting at my desk when the telephone rang. I did not recognize the name but the caller introduced himself as a headhunter. He asked whether I would consider joining another bank in a senior position. He took me to lunch to outline the proposal. There was intense pressure from the headhunter and I could not work out what to do. The attractions of moving were that it was a promotion and financially advantageous. Staying offered the opportunity to grow in a familiar environment in a company with integrity, along-side colleagues who knew both my faults and my strengths. Talking to anyone at work was obviously impossible. Despite my wife's support I felt very alone in trying to make a major life choice. I called three close friends from church who had some experience of the industry. They offered to meet almost immediately. We talked. I agonized and listened. We prayed. Over time they were able to help me straighten out my thinking. Often the short-term advantages, especially remuneration, can cloud our judgement – and friends can help cut through that by providing an objective viewpoint. Ultimately the choice and the responsibility for making the choice was mine, but I felt stronger for having talked. In the end, I stayed put, which was the right decision.

When I was 32, I found it very difficult to decide whether to ask Fi to marry me. When I prayed, it seemed that God was in the relationship and that he was asking me to take a step of faith, but whenever I reasoned, everything seemed unclear. I rang my father, who told me that a relationship was not a balance sheet, and I would there-fore never be able to balance the pros and cons! There were uncertainties that I could not give proper weight to. The idea of commitment frightened me. One evening we went to the opera. I still have the programme with most of the print on the cover wiped out from the sweat on my palms. We then went out for dinner. I had asked the waiter to have both Perrier and champagne available. The choice would depend on whether I would pluck up the courage to ask, and of course on what Fi's reply would be. She said yes, the champagne arrived and the relief was overwhelming. I felt on top of the world. Almost immediately, however, and for the only time in our marriage, I doubted the decision. The thought of lifelong commitment suddenly dawned on me. It all seemed too much and I wanted to run for cover. Forty-eight hours later, Fi and her family wanted to put an engagement announcement in the newspaper. I baulked at this idea, preferring to keep things a little more flexible! But deep down I knew the decision was right and there was little point in delaying. The announcement went in! This marked a point of no return, making a step of faith into a public act. Immediately afterwards, a huge peace came over me as I realized that God was in that decision. I have never looked back and we are fortunate to have a wonderful marriage.

Timing

You cannot squeeze a fruit ripe. The prophet Isaiah comments, 'I am the Lord; *in its time* I will do this swiftly' (Isaiah 60:22, italics mine). Often people struggle with the timing of answers to prayers for guidance. We ask ourselves, 'Why can't I just press a button and receive an immediate answer?' We want to fast-forward the video to the conclusion. But the fact is that our perceptions do not change immediately. We need time to distil and consider new insights, and often a clearer understanding of our motivations filters through the spectrum of everyday activities.

Even as a child I knew I could write. After a few career diversions where I became distracted by the appeal of earning regular money for such luxuries as rent and food, I finally committed myself to writing at the age of 30. Still enthralled to the concept of actually being paid for my work, I wrote anything that made money: jokes for radio shows, cheesy rhymes for greetings cards, terrible short stories for women's magazines. Eventually I returned to the idea of writing as a calling, a vocation, and began to take it more seriously.

There followed seven fruitless years as I attempted to write my Great Novel, win the Booker Prize, humbly receive the acclaim of the intellectual elite and take my rightful place in literary salons. As I sank into a financial abyss, I experienced every form of publisher's rejection from the tactful to the down-right insulting. Then it was time to take stock (the threatening letters from my bank manager played a valuable part in this decision). Taking a more realistic look at my life made me realise that I had confused the deceptively similar qualities of perseverance and stubbornness.

When I prayed I still believed that God wanted me to be a writer, but felt that my approach might have been wrong. Rather than give up and find a safe nine-to-five job where creativity was smothered at birth, I persevered – but changed my approach. By writing a lighter, more commercial novel, not only did I experience my first success but also the sense that this was what I had been created to do.

I was 40 when I had my first novel published and my sixth book is now due out this year. Perhaps the most telling comment came from a friend who said, 'When I read your books, I can hear your voice as clearly as if you were speaking to me in person.'

It wasn't the voice I had planned on communicating years ago but, she was right, it was *my* voice.

(Julie West, novelist)

If it seems that we are being led out of one job into another, it may take time for the groundwork to be prepared. We are sometimes restless for change but may lack the foundations that will sustain a changed set of circumstances. Often a first step is the loosening of the roots that attach us to a particular job. But over time we will also experience a quickening of our spirit in a positive sense, an inclination towards another job or another sector or another way of life. As the one slackens, so the other strengthens. We are not just called out of situations but we are called *in* to new openings and challenges. In 1 Corinthians 7:17, Paul tells us to, 'Retain the place in life that the Lord has assigned [you] and to which God has called [you].' The process of guidance is as important as the guidance itself. That's how we truly learn to trust and to listen.

Signs

Is it right to ask for God to give a guidance sign? Often the sign comes in the form of God-given peace, not just the sense of relief at a choice made, but a peace that passes understanding (Philippians 4:7). However, sometimes the sign is more unusual. Gideon laid a fleece before the Lord to test a decision (Judges 6:36–40). But it is important to note that the fleece was laid after the decision had been made – it was not a way of shirking responsibility. Requests for signs should be confirmatory rather than predictive and need only be made in special cases.

About one year after I became a Christian, I felt that
God was calling me out of my management consultant's job, and in to working full-time for my church.
The leaders of the church were very keen for me to
join the staff, but the problem was there was no
immediate opening, or budget to pay me. It was July,
and we agreed to review the situation later in the
year when the next year's budget was being drawn
up.

As time went on I felt that my heart was no longer
in my job and it didn't seem fair not to reveal my
plans to my boss (let's call him Ben). I was fairly sure
that I'd soon either be working for my church or in
another ministry. On the other hand, I didn't yet
have a firm offer so in a sense there were no plans to
tell him. I started to doubt whether I had heard God
right, and I prayed each day that he would show me
the right time to tell Ben about my longer-term
intention.

I became convinced that the 'right time' would be
after Ben came back from holiday in September.
However on 11 August, just before he went on holiday, he called a surprise meeting with me to tell me
that he was confused. On the one hand, he said I was
doing great work. On the other, he was disturbed
because he felt that my heart wasn't in the job. 'So,'

he said, 'the question I have is: do you really want to
do this job?' My heart was pounding as I thought,
'Well Lord, I suppose this must be the right time,
but it's not how I planned it!' So I told him, and we
agreed in about five minutes flat when and how I
would leave the company. Ben was understanding
and supportive, and offered to give me freelance
work to bridge any time elapsing between leaving the
consultancy and finding my new position.

An hour later, I was sitting alone in the office, in a
state of mild shock. It had all happened so quickly.
The cat was out of the bag, and suddenly I was head-
ing for a very different life. But was this really God's
will, or just a nice idea that I and a few others had
dreamed up? I got out my Bible and asked God to
please speak to me about this. This had been a really
tough week as I'd been dealing with a very difficult
situation in my family. If this was God's will, why had
he chosen today, of all days, to bring the situation to
a head?

My Bible opened at Amos chapter 8 and two
verses leapt out at me immediately. The first, verse 2:
'The time is ripe for my people Israel.' The second,
verse 9: 'In that day . . . I will make the sun go down
at noon and darken the earth in broad daylight.'

On that day, 11 August 1999, there had been a

total eclipse of the sun just before noon. To me, this
was a most wonderful sign of God's presence in the
decision and action I'd just taken.

(Pippa Richards, church worker)

Strategies and goals – how do we achieve our ambitions?

The musician Artur Schnabel was said to be one of the
great pianists because he could keep the architecture of an
entire sonata in his mind while playing every single note.
In Stephen Covey's book, *The Seven Habits of Highly Effective People*, he urges us to start with the end in mind. He
writes, 'If the ladder is not leaning against the right wall,
every step we take gets us to the wrong place faster.'
Settling a long view puts our day-to-day work in context. I
always advise those who are uncertain about their jobs to
treat the work that they are doing as if it were permanent,
thus ensuring a long-term attitude. It is also helpful to
break up long-term goals into shorter-term objectives.
These will need to be reviewed regularly, as our ambitions
rarely run along predictable tracks. However, they are still
useful, as they are closer in the line of sight and more
attainable. For example, to achieve the objective of becoming a director, we have to be prepared to reach our goal in
stages. This may mean changing departments strategically,

selecting training courses with our goal in mind, and consciously learning management skills from those to whose job we aspire.

Steady progress builds the confidence to deal with the inevitable setbacks. In Deuteronomy 7:22–23, Moses speaks to the Israelites about the Promised Land: 'The Lord your God will drive out those nations before you, little by little. You will not be allowed to eliminate them all at once, or the wild animals will multiply around you. But the Lord your God will deliver them over to you . . .' To reach our objectives, we often take on too much without being fully prepared. As we proceed in stages, we can eliminate obstacles as we go.

After five years in my job I was overlooked for promotion. I felt very let down and wondered whether the senior management were trying to tell me something. Finally I decided that commitment to any organization is a two-way street, imposing obligations on both employer and employee. I decided to stay. Careers seldom progress in direct upward lines, but rather in steps and plateaux. I became more focused in my work, setting myself the goal of being promoted next time. Ambitions are seldom fulfilled without setbacks, but setbacks are the very springboards for achievement.

Sometimes we need a paradigm shift in our thinking. We need to think outside of the box. The chairman of a

European airline company told me that his experience of turning the airline around had been rather like persuading people to run through a brick wall, which they then discovered was made of papier mâché. It may be that your particular brick wall is thinner than you think, and once broken, might even be a door of opportunity.

Destruction and deception – how do we avoid the dangers?

Lives can be destroyed by ambition that gets out of control. At the end of Shakespeare's play, *King Henry VIII,* Cardinal Wolsey says to Thomas Cromwell on his deathbed:

> Had I but served my God with half the zeal
> I served my King, he would not in mine age
> Have left me naked to mine enemies.

When our ambition becomes divorced from the context of extending God's kingdom, it risks destroying us. In Wolsey's case, serving King Henry VIII took over from serving God. Similarly, our career can easily become an end in itself if we lose sight of its real purpose. We need to keep acknowledging God as the source of our goals and the director of our lives.

I know people whose ambitions have got out of control

and destroyed their families and their businesses as well as themselves. A distinguished consultant told me of the warning signs to watch for: suspicion of other people bordering on paranoia; satisfaction when others fail; indulging in character assassination; introspective behaviour; an inability to receive advice or love; egocentricity and the conviction that one is always right; and chronic dissatisfaction with one's life. We need to remember that 'The heart is deceitful above all things' (Jeremiah 17:9). Therefore, if we are to hold our ambition lightly and avoid self-deception, we need to ask the Holy Spirit to show us our true intentions. We also need to be accountable to those around us whom we know and trust.

The following questions can be helpful pointers for career direction: Do I have confidence while praying and worshipping that God is setting the agenda, or are there persistent niggles? Is my ambition so personal that I don't want to talk about it? This can be a tell-tale sign of self-indulgence. Do other people believe that God is in this vision even if they don't fully grasp it? If we are satisfied with the answers to these questions, that is a positive sign.

Donald Bradman, one of the greatest cricketers of all time, used to hit a golf ball with a cricket stump regularly to perfect his eye. Once he had perfected this, it became relatively easy to hit the bigger ball with a wider cricket bat. In our generation, commitment and 'stickability' are in short supply, but we need discipline and perseverance in pursuit of our God-given ambitions. Jesus was ambitious to complete the work that God had sent him to do (John 4:34). He listened to the Father constantly and focused entirely on his mission. His last gasp on the cross was, 'It is finished' (John 19:30). Our aim should also be to complete the task he has set for us and so to reflect Jesus in our God-given callings.

More than ever before we need Christians with ambition in the workplace. People who will set demanding challenges for themselves but who will also recognize that true ambition cannot be achieved individually. We are to be accountable to others and hold others to account. We also need to break the perception that God prefers us to settle into being low achievers, or we will fail to make an impact on our communities. Paul strained forward to achieve fully an ambition that God gave him. This conviction sustained him throughout every imaginable adversity and enabled him in the end to say he had 'fought the good fight', and had 'finished the race' (2 Timothy 4:7). That should be our life's mission.

Tough Decisions

Today, we have more knowledge than ever before: we have access to databases, we can surf the net, we can communicate across continents – but the task of making tricky decisions is no easier. We can almost not live without Google. If knowledge is out there, it is instantly accessible. We are long on knowledge but short on wisdom. How then do we make wise, tough decisions at work?

A senior stockbroker told me that it was not possible to hold a general moral view of the workplace. Harsh choices had to be made, compromises reached and truth had at times to be 'qualified' because we lived in the real commercial world where everyone knew the game and would not be dealing 'as if the workplace were a church'. Special rules therefore had to be applied to the business world.

I have never accepted this. Medical ethics, cyber ethics, and business ethics describe different areas of choice with differing complexities but the choices are all based on the same objective biblical standard. There are right and wrong choices. One of the richest men in the world, King

Solomon, prayed for 'a discerning heart to govern your people and to distinguish between right and wrong' (1 Kings 3:9). All the invented terms such as 'inappropriate' and 'counterproductive' are efforts to avoid the simple ethical fact that there is a right and wrong course of action which should, without embarrassment, be described as such. This does not mean that there are instant obvious answers to complex moral questions. On the contrary, there is frequently a process to go through as we reach a conclusion. When seeking a compass through the confusing maze of commercial decisions I have found four ways of reaching a decision helpful. First, our relationship with God provides the context for all our decisions. We look to the Bible, which provides a moral framework for our actions. Second, we have God-given faculties of reasoning underlined throughout the Bible, and demonstrated by the prophet Isaiah's call: 'Come now, let us reason together' (Isaiah 1:18). Third, we are given what Augustine called 'a kind of silent clamour of truth ringing inside' – our conscience. This is the Spirit prodding us in a God-ward direction. Last, we need to assess the consequences of our decisions not only for ourselves, but also the effect on others. The best decisions are made when these are aligned.

Decisions and values – how to be consistent

Making tough decisions is one of the most crucial issues in the workplace. We need to be clear, robust and determined in making our choices. Of course, everyone makes decisions based, sometimes unconsciously, on a set of values. There is often a tacit assumption at work that we all share a set of common values, but this may not be the case.

A client asked me to pass some vital information about his business to the underwriter. I forgot to pass it on, resulting in a very restrictive decision from the underwriter regarding my client's insurance policy and a very annoyed client. My initial reaction was to hide the fact that this was my mistake. It would have been easy to pass it off as the underwriter's neglect and I spent a while trying to work out the best way to do this. However, as I did so, I became aware of a growing sense of shame. I realized, having prayed under my breath, that the only thing to do was to risk the client's anger and tell him that the mistake was mine. So I rang him and confessed. His response surprised me: 'Don't worry – if you never make mistakes, that just shows that you never do anything.' I have learnt a lot from this one, and have become more confident about living out my values in the work-place.

(Paul Groves, insurance broker)

At the heart of all business scandals is an individual person exercising a judgement both of what is right and wrong but also, sadly, of what can be got away with. There is a need for regulation, but these rules of the game are merely a guide and not a substitute for a set of faith-based values. Like our faith, our values will affect our decisions in every area of our lives. In this sense there is no distinction between so-called personal decisions and work-related decisions. Integrity is the word we use when our actions are aligned with our principles and there is no disconnection. This comes into sharp focus when the values that public figures live by are seen to differ from those they promote. We cannot compartmentalize our lives into a private sphere and a professional sphere, with separate rules for each.

A few years ago I went to Italy representing my company on a trip organized by a major client. One evening ten of us (all men) went out for dinner and then on to a club. It became clear that the guy organizing the evening had laid on female escorts for all of us at the next venue. As I realized what was happening, I had to act very quickly to avoid being

carried along by the crowd and into the next taxi.
I subtly escaped to the gents and called my wife for
some moral support and time to think. Then I was
able to catch a taxi back to the hotel. The next
morning I definitely felt excluded. One guy commented to me, 'Whatever plays away stays away' and
I felt he was looking for reassurance that I wouldn't
spill the beans. Others gave the impression that they
found my non-participation slightly pathetic. Still
others, I think, felt judged. All in all, though it was
the right thing to do, it had an adverse effect on my
relationship with these people, in some cases long-
term. However, one guy who noticed my stance has
recently sought opportunities to work with me.

(Alex Lee, finance director)

Practical steps – how do we make wise choices?

1. Follow the wisdom of God

Wisdom is knowing and doing what is right and comes
from God. In his introduction to Proverbs, Eugen Peterson, the translator of *The Message*, the Bible in contemporary language, describes wisdom:

Wisdom is the biblical term for this on-earth-as-it-is-
in-heaven everyday living. Wisdom is the art of living

skilfully in whatever actual conditions we find ourselves. It has virtually nothing to do with information
as such, with knowledge as such. A college degree is
no certification of wisdom – nor is it primarily con-
cerned with keeping us out of moral mud puddles,
although it does have a profound moral effect upon
us. Wisdom has to do with becoming skilful in hon-
ouring our parents and raising our children, handling
our money and conducting our sexual lives, going to
work and exercising leadership, using words well and
treating friends kindly, eating and drinking healthily,
cultivating emotions within ourselves and attitudes
toward others that make for peace. Threaded through
all these items is the insistence that the way we think
of and respond to God is the most practical thing we
do. In matters of everyday practicality, nothing,
absolutely nothing, takes precedence over God.

Through reading the Bible regularly and meditating on
God's truth, we build up reservoirs of wisdom and form
a biblical world view. Our own reflections can be supple-
mented by reading about other Christians, whose experiences provide useful case studies of God's actions in
different situations. Building strong foundations in this
way stands us in good stead for moments when we need to
make difficult decisions and stops us frantically thumbing

through our Bible as if it were Google, desperately looking for a quick answer.

When facing a critical choice our first response should be to step back. It can be difficult to create space when a dominant issue is at the forefront of our mind. I recommend that people facing a very major decision take two days out to seek God. Day one is simply to chill out. It is amazing how draining it is to confront a looming decision. A break to restore physical strength is therefore essential. During day two it is better not to pray constantly about the particular decision. Rather, use the time to meditate on who God is, on his ways in the world generally and his overall plans for his people. This search for a wider context alleviates the acute pressure caused by constantly churning a decision around in our minds. It also widens the perspective and enables the decision to be made from a broader point of view – God's point of view. We need constant reminders that his thoughts are not our thoughts, nor his ways our ways (Isaiah 55:8).

2. Make the complex simple
Our ability to make tough decisions improves with our technical competence.

I work in child protection, and the most difficult decision I face is to decide when a child needs to be removed from his or her home. I had one particularly complex case, which I agonized over for some time. My decision was subsequently challenged in court, which I found very stressful, but eventually the court backed my judgment and supported my decision. I realized that I did actually have the necessary skills to do my job and make these decisions. It's never easy, but I feel more confident as a result of the court case.

(Vanessa Clark, social worker)

We do need to understand the technicalities of our job, but there is a real temptation to confuse technical complexity with the underlying fundamental choices. In the words of General Omar Bradley, 'We have become a nation of technological giants and moral pygmies.'

When I have to make a difficult decision at work, I try to reduce it to its simplest form. It can be helpful to write down the issue, using the minimum number of words. Most complex decisions have, at their root, simple, albeit difficult, choices. It takes time to see the real choice in its stark simplicity, stripped of mountains of fact, others' opinions, our own reflections and confused motivation. How often does one hear in a meeting, 'But the *real* question is . . .'?

3. *Listen to the question*

In our day-to-day work, we have to deal with a range of questions. It is therefore instructive to see how Jesus dealt with three different and difficult questions in Luke chapter 20. In the first case, Jesus is teaching the people in the temple. The senior community leaders approach him and ask, 'Tell us by what authority you are doing these things . . . Who gave you this authority?' (Luke 20:2). Jesus, of course, sees that they are trying to trick him and replies by asking a question: 'Tell me, John's baptism – was it from heaven, or from [human origin]?' (Luke 20:3–4). The questioners are now caught in a dilemma. If they say 'from heaven', then why didn't they believe him? But if they reply 'of human origin', they fear being stoned because John was generally thought to be a prophet. They prevaricate, answering, 'We don't know where it was from' (Luke 20:7). Jesus therefore declined to answer their question. Not every question has to be answered. It is important to remember this, for example, when conducting a negotiation on behalf of a client. An unfair question, such as, 'Is this really your client's final offer?' is usually best avoided by saying something like, 'This is the offer that is on the table for your consideration'.

In the second case Jesus gives an extremely adroit answer. The teachers of the law and the chief priests send spies to try to catch Jesus out. They say to him, 'Teacher, we know that you speak and teach what is right, and that you do not show partiality but teach the way of God in accordance with the truth. Is it right for us to pay taxes to Caesar or not?' (Luke 20:21–22). In the first sentence the spies butter him up. It is like the salesman sitting in a meeting and hearing a customer say, 'I think this is the best product we have ever seen. It does everything for us. It is so good, our clients just can't wait to get more of it.' Then comes the sting in the tail: 'But the price . . .' In Jesus' story the sting is the question, 'Is it right for us to pay taxes to Caesar or not?' It is set up so that Jesus will either be accused of treason (if he says taxes should not be paid) or seen as an oppressor of the people for siding with Caesar (if he says they should). Jesus avoids both. He asks them for a coin and points out Caesar's portrait, replying, 'Then give to Caesar what is Caesar's, and to God what is God's' (Luke 20:25). Just because we are presented with a polarity of the questioner's own choice, we do not have to restrict our answers to the options offered. In a work situation we often feel forced into a yes or no answer when the issue is best approached from a different angle.

Third, the Sadducees ask a particularly complicated question about a woman with seven husbands, enquiring whose wife she will be when she gets to heaven (Luke 20:27–33). It is a difficult but honest question and Jesus gives them a helpful and clear reply. When the real object of the question is to elicit a straight answer, then one should be given.

So to three different kinds of questions we hear three different kinds of answers. The first is a trick question which Jesus does not answer. The second is a complex question set up to be a trap, which Jesus discerns and avoids. The third is an honest question that gets an honest answer. We need the help of the Holy Spirit to discern the nature of the question.

It is important not to ask a question if you are unable to handle the answer. I was told by a client the story of Robert McNamara, who was Secretary of State in America at the time of the Cuban Missile Crisis and was reflecting on a conversation with Andre Gromyko, the Foreign Minister of Russia. McNamara had deliberately avoided the direct question, 'Are there nuclear missiles on Cuba?' He was confident the Foreign Minister would not lie to him and that therefore the answer would be 'Yes'. A positive reply might well have led to an immediate attack. He wisely did not ask the question because the implications of the answer were too hot to handle – the crisis was averted and perhaps this restraint contributed to the outcome. The rich young politician in Luke asked Jesus what he could do to inherit eternal life. He could not handle the reply to sell all and give it to the poor, and he left disappointed.

4. Consider the consequences

Many tough decisions that have to be made each day in the workplace require us to measure the short-term implications against the longer-term. So, for example, spending money in the short-term might be painful, but in the longer-term the investment could well pay off. Decisions are destroyed by 'short-termism'. We need to cultivate the habit of making immediate tough decisions in the light of future circumstances. Jesus said, 'Suppose one of you wants to build a tower. Will [you] not first sit down and estimate the cost to see if [you have] enough money to complete it?' (Luke 14:28).

When we are making a difficult decision we should manage the downside risk and let the upside take care of itself. Too much time is usually spent thinking about the potential benefits when it is the potential cost of things going wrong that needs most careful attention. The impact of our decisions on other people should also be considered.

Last year my business reached the point where I could no longer avoid making some of my workforce redundant. It was a very, very painful experience, one of the toughest decisions I ever made. I was constrained by the requirements of employment law but tried to be both fair and compassionate to each individual. I prayed that each one would quickly find a new job that would suit their gifting and meet their family's financial needs.

(Ray Wilkinson, HR manager)

5. Implement the strategy

Once we have made a decision, we need to think about the best way to implement it. Our call as Christians is to be 'as shrewd as snakes and as innocent as doves' (Matthew 10:16). How hard it is to do that, especially as I believe that we are called to live this way at the *same* time. In the parable of the shrewd manager (Luke 16:1–9), the manager is shrewd yet dishonest, but only his shrewdness is commended. Our challenge is to be shrewd, by which I mean streetwise, clever or strategic, while at the same time being honest. When Daniel was taken to the Babylonian court, he resolved not to defile himself with the non-kosher royal food and wine given by the king (Daniel 1). However, rather than giving a flat refusal, he approached the chief official for permission to have a vegetarian diet instead. Daniel knew that the official would be executed if those in his charge did not look well. Rather than force a confrontation, he suggested a trial period of ten days. The special diet would only continue if they all looked well. By considering the situation from the official's point of view, taking his concerns seriously and providing a pragmatic course of action, Daniel was able to get what he wanted. God blessed him and made him stronger than any of the others.

Profit and responsibility – can we have both?

One of the difficult areas for decision is how to balance the needs of the wider communities in which businesses operate with the pursuit of profit. For many, the idea that a corporation should try to embrace a wider agenda is a breach of a fundamental understanding of the need to maximize profit for the benefit of shareholders. But increasingly there is recognition of the importance of the wider perspective, alongside a necessarily strong defence of profit. After all, only profitable, efficient firms will have the added value to share more widely. The twin of rights is duties. Too often we assert our rights but neglect the acceptance of a reciprocal duty. Employers recognize that it is not just shareholders, but also consumers, customers, pensioners and the community in which the corporation operates who are stakeholders and who are affected by corporate decisions.

My own view is that properly developed corporate responsibility, far from being a drag on profitability, is essential to long-term stability. If major corporations act responsibly and out of a sense of being good global citizens, much of the friction caused by relations between the developing and developed world will be mitigated. If we wish to spread the benefits of globalization as widely as possible, free trade will also need to become fair trade. The failure of the World Trade Organization to deal with the subsidies given by developed nations to their own exporters and the tariffs imposed on the developing world when seeking markets in developed countries is deeply offensive.

A robust concern for the environment is also key. The beginning of Genesis makes it clear that God has made human beings stewards of the material resources of the earth. I would argue that the capitalist system, with all its faults, is still the best system for utilizing these resources, but efficiency should not outweigh sustainability. These issues of corporate responsibility are relevant for all employees, not just those in positions of senior executive authority. Often I'm told, 'It's OK for you, but no one will listen to me.' All employers want their businesses to be thought of as places of excellence and best practice. Increasingly there are representative groups and committees where it would be appropriate for employees at every level to raise these matters. The more concern that is shown for these issues, the more responsive management will become to them. The culture is changing and the time has come to draw together the short-term requirements of the market place with some of the more important long-term effects of globalization.

It is important for all employees to know that they are valued, irrespective of their gender, marital status, nationality, faith, background or sexual orientation. Diversity provides a range of different perspectives, which brings a better balance of judgement to a team. We are all made in the image of God and therefore have something to offer. When Christ came, he broke down the barriers that divide people (Ephesians 2:14), and working together is one way of living this out. It is also important for employees to be able to respect the values of their organization.

For me it has been an enormous advantage to work for a bank which has consistently set integrity as its hallmark. I have always known that my values will be given a fair hearing and evaluated on their merits. When I was a junior executive, I remember a debate about whether it was appropriate to sponsor the financing of a series of clinics primarily focused on abortion. Instinctively I felt it was wrong but I knew that others disagreed. The simple option was to say nothing, but I decided to speak to the chairman and explain the level of my concerns, which related both to my personal morality and to the reputation of the bank. To my surprise he thought that it was appropriate to raise both aspects. At the critical meeting I prayed that we would not have to make the decision, and thus be forced into division. The proposal fell away for an apparently unrelated reason: but it was right to raise the issue. Of course not every moral issue has to be fought with the same moral intensity. Defective work practices often require time and patient argument to be corrected. Discernment is needed in order to know when to press an issue and when to stay silent. Above all, respect for others who have a different point of view should be paramount.

Patterns of living – who shapes them?
We are overwhelmed by choices in everyday life. It is an essential part of our spiritual journey that we learn to make difficult choices and then to live with their consequences. Making decisions is a prime part of our maturing as people. We don't always get it right, however hard we may have prayed and sought God's help – we are human and not divine. And yes, we rejoice in getting judgements right, but let us not forget that we cannot gain experience without making mistakes and taking wrong decisions. But wisdom is greater than experience. And we only grow in wisdom if we learn from our mistakes. Siegmund Warburg, my first boss, said on this subject: 'Some name it disappointment and become poorer, others name it experience and become richer.'

Our decisions should be made from the perspective of lives lived for God and not just for our own enjoyment.

Paul, writing to the Romans, urges us not to let the pressures from the world shape our pattern of living. He gives this summary, which I have found foundational to my decision-making:

> So here is what I want you to do, God helping you: take your everyday, ordinary life – your sleeping, eating, going-to-work, and walking-around life – and place it before God as an offering. Embracing what God does for you is the best thing you can do for him. Don't become so well-adjusted to your culture that you fit into it without even thinking. Instead, fix your attention on God. You will be changed from the inside out. Readily recognize what he wants from you, and quickly respond to it. Unlike the culture around you, always dragging you down to its level of immaturity, God brings the best out of you, develops well-formed maturity within you. (Romans 12:1–2, *The Message*.)

Work–Life Balance

How often do you hear the frustrated cry, 'I haven't got enough time'? The pressure to do an increasing number of activities more and more rapidly is all-pervasive, but we do not become holy by working harder. There are proper restraints that need to be placed upon our work. Work–life balance is now at the top of many personnel departments' agenda. It is clear that the demands made on people to devote huge amounts of time to work for an undefined period are unsustainable. The owner of a large international French-based spirits company told me that he had offered his employees the opportunity to exchange the notoriously long French holidays for a lump sum in cash. While those in their forties accepted the offer at once, those in their twenties rejected it. A younger generation is increasingly and rightly seeking a lifestyle which balances life in the workplace and outside it.

Competing demands – what should our priorities be?

Priorities are essential if we are to achieve our ambitions and at the same time hold on to our values. I believe that the right order of priorities is God, our core relationships and the work that God has called us to. For most people, core relationships will either be spouse and children or close friendships, and the work that God has called them to will primarily be their jobs, but may include other God-given activities. It is also important to rest.

I was in charge of the emerging market debt financing business for a large investment bank in London. My main focus was on Latin America. I really loved my work as it brought me into contact with very senior people in governments and companies in these emerging countries. Although the travelling and working hours were demanding, it was worthwhile. I felt we were contributing to the economic development of these countries.

One afternoon I received some very exciting news at work. We had made it to the final stages of a bidding contest for a $200 million financing for a Brazilian company, our first in that country. We stood to make substantial fees and establish our

credentials in a huge market that we had not yet
cracked. I rushed home to spend a bit of time with
my wife and our three-month-old baby girl. A
lengthy conference call was scheduled at 8pm with
the board of the Brazilian company. I was going to
explain our proposed strategy for raising the money
and answer a barrage of questions. Half an hour later
they would choose the bank they wanted to work
with. I arrived home full of excitement, only to have
my wife hand me the baby and her bottle.

'Here,' she said. 'I'm so glad you're on time
because I need to go to my dinner right away.'

'What dinner?'

'You know, Gill [her boss] is in town from San
Francisco for just one day and we're having dinner
with all of the staff. Don't tell me you forgot.'

'I forgot,' I said sheepishly. 'And I have a call with
the Brazilians in an hour to finalize this deal. If I
can't be on the call, we'll lose the business.'

I felt like throwing a tantrum, but in all honesty I
knew it wasn't fair for Debs to be three hours late for
her dinner. I took Lily in my arms and prayed for
something to work out. I was not very hopeful.

Forty-five minutes later the telephone rang. I was
playing peek-a-boo with Lily. When I tried to start
the conference call, Lily started wailing at 85

decibels. I tried to get Sergio, the finance director, to pick up the phone so the others couldn't hear our conversation, but he would not take my hints.

'Sergio, I'm sorry I can't talk to you now. It is absolutely impossible,' I said, with two of my team in New York and another in Sao Paolo listening, as well as his entire board.

'Miles, you have to speak to us now. We are about to make our decision.'

'I can't. Is there any way we can delay?'

'No we can't! I told you this afternoon. What is the problem?'

'Uh,' I hesitated. Then I decided to tell the truth. 'I made a big mistake. My wife is out tonight – I completely forgot about a dinner she has with her boss. I really messed up. I am looking after my baby girl right now. She is crying so I really should go. I am terribly sorry for any disappointment this may have caused you. I understand that you have to make a decision soon and that I will not be able to make the contribution I had hoped to make.'

'Baby girl? What's her name?'

'Lily.'

'That's a pretty name.' I heard murmurs of approval in the background.

'Is that her crying right now?'

'Yes. I am so sorry about this.'

'Don't worry about it. How long do you need?'

'I'll put her to bed in about an hour.'

'Call us when she's asleep. We'll be here.'

I hung up, completely dumbfounded. I sang to Lily until she went to sleep, and then called the Brazilians. I did not dare to hook in my colleagues in New York because I feared their scathing criticism for being willing to blow a deal over a ridiculous babysitting problem. Sergio and the whole board were still there.

'Well, is she asleep?' he asked.

'Yes she is,' I replied, feeling like a complete idiot.

'That's good. OK, what do you want to tell us?'

I went through our proposal. It was the most amazing conversation. I put any thought of closing the deal out of my mind. All I wanted to do was help these people through their concerns and issues so that they could make the decision that worked best for their company. Eventually, they hung up to deliberate. Half an hour later they called me back to say we had won the business. I just sat there and looked at the phone. I left an embarrassed message for my colleagues in New York to start cranking up the machine, and went to bed, thanking God for helping me out.

(Miles Protter, Managing Partner of
The Values Partnership)

Early on in my working life, I found it hard to imagine what it would look like to be committed to my work and yet give my core relationships higher priority. A crunch point came when I found myself utterly absorbed in a very stimulating and confidential deal. I became so engrossed that I didn't speak to my wife, Fi, for a week. She was extremely patient but, not surprisingly, by the end of the week felt desperately neglected. I had to resist the temptation towards self-justification. As I did so, I knew that this was not the right way to live and I resolved that this would never happen again.

As I travel a great deal, I now try to speak to Fi every day, wherever I am in the world. I avoid waking her up wherever possible, but we have both decided that being woken is preferable to not speaking. The main point of the phone call is to show that Fi has my front of mind and heart attention, and for this it is important to stay in touch through a daily exchange of information.

I also try to stay in regular contact with my children, even if it is just a quick text message. Supporting whatever they are involved in, whether watching matches, concerts or debates is equally important. When I am in the middle of an impossibly busy period and it seems that I will never have the time or inclination to have fun again, this is the moment to put something in the diary. I remember taking the children and some friends of theirs to see Simon and

Garfunkel in the middle of a very busy period. At times, we need counterbalancing stimuli. We also need reminders of key relationships and the need to maintain them.

I appreciate the support of a small group of friends, which meets regularly to keep in touch and pray. I have also valued mentors over the years, generally older Christians, who have been kind enough to offer me their time and wisdom. I have limited interest in listening to work–life balance theories, but I do want to learn from those who are engaging with the issue, and making progress. We all need to help each other. It is experience and not the textbook that makes the difference.

Yes or no – how do we decide?

The writer Arnold Bennett remarked, 'We shall never have more time. We have, and always have had, all the time there is.' Who is the master of time? Either time imposes its tyranny on our lives or we act decisively, using it to reflect our priorities. Instead of trying to slot God into a predispositioned spreadsheet of our own making, we need to shape our lives into his patterns because we realize these are good for us. We need to exercise the authority that God has given us over time, recognizing the forces that distract us from fulfilling God's purposes. At a breakfast meeting with a new business developer for a multinational corporation, I remember discussing the issue of planning. He travels a lot with his job, but he told me that he tries to organize his time so that he is at home at weekends to see his family and on Tuesday evenings to go to the church group he and his wife feel called to lead together. This involves a bit of planning and sometimes leaving for work on some very late night flights after the group has ended.

I remember the story of the best banker of his generation, Sir Siegmund Warburg. His secretary rushed in to tell him that the Chancellor of the Exchequer was on the telephone and said it was urgent. Sir Siegmund's reply was instructive: 'Urgent for whom? For him or for me?' This was perhaps a little arrogant but it proves a point. As stewards of time we need to step back and ensure that we are not merely whirled along by the exigencies of the moment. The urgent is often the enemy of the important.

The story of Jesus in John 11:1–16 is very telling. His great friend Lazarus was sick and on the point of death. Every instinct in him must have been telling him to go and see his friend. But Jesus waited and did not rush off immediately as his disciples would have urged him to do. In due course, he decided the time was right to go. But at first he held back. At times we need to check powerful and natural emotions in order to achieve God-given objectives. The first gut reaction is not necessarily the right course of action. Jesus knew the bigger picture and ultimately he was able to glorify God by going at the right time and raising Lazarus from the dead.

Jesus only did what he saw the Father doing (John 5:19). In our work the temptation can be to try to do more than God is doing. I often have to remind myself that I can only do what God's will is for me, and no more. Restraint is an important understanding of priority. We need to say no in order to be able to say yes.

A few years ago, I was asked to be a trustee of a major charity. I loved the people involved and believed in their vision. I was flattered by the request and everything within me was ready to say yes. However, while praying, I felt a lingering uncertainty. The balance of work and other commitments meant that reluctantly I had to say no. It is hard to say no when you want to say yes. But 'no' to one thing often opens the way to another. Subsequent events proved the decision right, as the time commitment would have been far greater than originally anticipated, and more than I could have managed.

Learning to refuse the excessive demands of the workplace can feel daunting. Many of us feel we need a worthy excuse such as a family wedding or a pre-booked weekend away to justify saying no to extra work. However, when we take a step back, all of us can see that rest is essential. I aim for at least a day a week when I switch off from the creative activity of my mainstream work. Keeping one day free of work is healthy – we should respect it but not be bound legalistically by it (Mark 2:27). Like many others I sometimes have to spend Sunday working, but it is important that this happens by exception and not because we are failing to plan our work, falling into bad habits, or becoming ill-disciplined in our work patterns. Learning to work efficiently, and without time wasting, is an important biblical principle that enables us to develop the necessary discipline to become good stewards of time. Most companies know the negative impact of making ill-considered demands on employees. When it does occur, a well-reasoned discussion with a manager is a good approach.

Balance often needs two people to strike the pivotal point. Making our concerns known with a direct but positive attitude often has the benefit not only of resolving a particular work–life imbalance but of affecting working practices for the good, thus benefiting other colleagues.

Compulsions and addictions – how can we break free?

To many today the word 'idol' is associated with the cult of celebrity, something benign like 'Pop Idol'. However, in the Bible, an idol is anything that pushes God out of our lives. Compulsions and addictions such as workaholism or alcoholism, shopping binges, pornography and recreational drugs are all idols. Only God can break the power of destructive habits and bring balance to our lives.

I remember praying with a young stockbroker at the end of a church service. He reluctantly told me that he was addicted to cocaine. He felt that there had to be more to life but God seemed inaccessible. We talked about the fact that on the cross Jesus broke the power of evil, including all compulsions and addictions. When I prayed for him, the Holy Spirit came upon him with extraordinary power, causing him to shake visibly. He subsequently joined a home group and although at times it was a struggle to stay clean, the drug dependency was broken, leaving him free to live a fulfilled and balanced life.

A senior executive told me that his greatest struggle as a Christian was his reliance on work to give meaning to his life. Workaholism can be as acute an addiction as any recreational substance. As we talked we discovered that many of the root causes of his issue seemed to lie in his childhood, where he was under constant pressure to achieve. Somehow, whatever he did was not good enough for his father. We prayed together and he accepted that there was a problem, thus clearing the decks for a life strategy. He knew that if he did not bring his addiction under control, it could well destroy his life and his marriage, and he decided to take responsibility for restoring the balance. We agreed on some strategies, including not taking papers and problems home, working efficiently during the day, not talking about work to his wife for a period, and practising doing nothing. He found the latter the most difficult of all, but started to keep Sundays free not only from work, but also from thinking about work. Gradually he started to realize that he did not need to work to be valued by God. Jesus heard the Father's voice saying 'You are my Son, whom I love; with you I am well pleased' (Luke 3:22) before any of his public work had begun. Love precedes work.

Over the years I have had the privilege to observe that as the overall balance of this senior executive's life has changed, he has become fulfilled and at ease in his relationships not only at home but particularly at work. In an interview in *Fortune* (November 2002), Daniel Vassela, the chief executive of one of the largest pharmaceutical companies in the world – Novartis – was asked about money and motivation:

The strange part is this, the more I made, the more I got preoccupied with money. When suddenly I didn't have to think about money as much, I found myself starting to think increasingly about it. Money corrupts the mind. By the same token, you can find yourself in a situation where you worry more and more about your reputation and become its prisoner

. . . It is wrong to worry about whether you will be the hero next month. One day, the glitter will be gone anyway.

I remember talking to a 25-year-old banker who had just received a big bonus and realized that he had become more absorbed with the money than he had expected. Peter writes in his second letter (2 Peter 2:19) that people are slaves to whatever has mastered them. A love of money or power can grow almost imperceptibly until we find ourselves enslaved. My own experience is that freedom from such captivity requires daily discipline. We need to recognize and be grateful for God's hand in what we have achieved, and not be afraid to use our money, reputation and skill for his purposes. But we also need to pray regularly for the power of God's Spirit to dethrone idols that rob us of our freedom.

Freedom and discipline – how do we get the trend line right?

In practice it is not possible to lead a perfectly balanced life all the time. There are phases in many careers which demand long hours: for example, the early years of medicine. In addition, all of us have times when the demands of work outstrip our desire to live balanced lives.

The barrister in a difficult trial will be consumed for a number of weeks on the issues. A business trip may take us away for a period. At other times family life will be of critical importance: for example, when a baby is born, a child starts a new school or someone close to us is sick. But what is important is not the oscillations but the trend. Is it directionally right, even if momentarily out of line? For example, if the trend line shows an excess of time spent on church activities, then it should be corrected in the next period to allow for more time at work or with family.

Within a well-organized schedule we must also allow time for sudden changes of pace. New projects arrive unexpectedly or God intervenes in our lives in a way that needs a response. If we don't have flexibility, our life can be driven by fixed priorities and burdensome milestones. The Spirit of God brings freedom within a framework. This is the balance we seek. Jesus talks to those who are burnt out and urges them to discover 'the unforced rhythms of grace' (Matthew 11:29, *The Message*). We each need to work out a style of time management that suits us. The test is this: Does the structure free us or trap us?

We should review our diaries rigorously: how much time have I spent productively? How much has been wasted? Have I given myself enough time to rest? Have I managed to spend regular time alone with God? Can I see what God is blessing and then resource it with time, energy and money? Often these questions are easier to answer with the help of some close friends. With God, we try to draw the right line, realizing that mistakes will be made along the way. The diary review is good because the record does not lie. It tells it as it is. The next step is to try to plan the forward diary to reflect your chosen lifestyle values. If you constantly fail the diary audit, then it's time to think again. Something is out of kilter in your life.

Stop and think – review to renew

If we are on the highway of God's purposes it is a waste of time constantly to be looking for the exit or worrying as to whether we are on track. We need not worry daily whether a previous decision is the right one or what the next move should be. It is in this sense that Jesus warns us that we should take care of each day as it comes, for it has problems of its own, and not to fret about tomorrow (Matthew 6:34). However, many people carry on doing the same work uncritically. They stay busy but bored. To avoid this, all of us need to review our lives from time to time, for example on key birthdays or at regular set intervals.

Each year I had an annual appraisal as part of my pay review process. I found this was very helpful in terms of recognizing what I had learnt and achieved to date and seeing where I wanted to go. Preparing for my review one year, I realized that I was in the wrong career. I looked at my senior colleagues, their lifestyle, responsibilities and ambitions – and realized I did not want their jobs. I am glad to have been given the opportunity to stop and think about my work from a professional standpoint and would counsel an annual review to everyone. I did have to wait a few years before I was called into something new, but the review helped me to see where my strengths and passions lie.

(Julie Brant, solicitor)

Sometimes fundamental doubts about what we are doing hit us unexpectedly. There are times – hitting the big numbers such as 30, 40, or 50 – when it is right to re-assess one's career and check up on the many crosswinds that can drive us off-course from our original objectives. I remember after several years in the same job being involved in the battle for control of Harrods – one of the most hard fought battles in UK corporate history. We were advising the company, which was being attacked by another company headed by Tiny Rowland. It was a lengthy and exhausting transaction and I found myself questioning whether I really wanted to spend the rest of my life working to achieve the corporate objectives of others. I re-opened a book I thought I had closed and again asked whether I might be called to a full-time preaching ministry. I concluded that this should not be dismissed as a consequence of stress but that it was a proper question that went deeper.

I re-analysed the reasons why I was in my current job and spoke to a prominent Christian leader who knew me well. I was surprised by the strength of his reaction as he advised me to stay where I was. He pointed out that my original sense of God's calling was unchanged, and questioned whether I had just hit what he called the 'middle patch', when doubts typically arise. He pointed me to St Paul's view 'for God's gifts and his call are irrevocable' (Romans 11:29). He also reminded me that the church was abundantly endowed with preachers but had very few bankers.

At about the same time, I decided to fast and pray about my future. I was still wondering whether I should stay in finance. I had reflected, analysed, talked to my wife and close friends. I went for a walk along the Thames and decided to read the last chapter of Luke and the beginning of Acts. As I read, I had an extraordinary sense of release, the fog of uncertainty cleared and one verse leapt out at me: 'Stay in the city until you have been clothed with power from on high' (Luke 24:49). The immediate circumstances to which this verse refers were wholly different to mine, but I had no doubt then, and have no doubt now, that this was God's whispered encouragement for me to stay working in the City of London. I also began to see in a new way that God seeks obedience more than sacrifice. At times, I think the idea of making a sacrifice for God by leaving my career appealed to me, but as I read Acts 5:32, I realized that God gives the Holy Spirit not purely inspirationally, but to those who *obey* him. I had assumed that the time had come when I would be filled with the Spirit for a new ministry and would leave the City. I was mistaken. In the years thereafter it has become clear that God gives us the power of the Spirit to equip us both for day-to-day work and, if he calls us to it, a wider ministry.

Twin track – success and significance

As part of the struggle to balance our lives, many people decide to change their lifestyle and move to less stressful jobs. These downshifting moves offer greater opportunities for leisure, but they are not a cure-all and often do not add that key dimension to a successful working life: not just more leisure, but significance. Most of us would like to experience the satisfaction of being involved with people who make change happen. We often look at our lives –

usually at the lowest point – and then compare it to some specially significant vocational calling. Significance is not something achieved late in life after giving up a full-time job. Our aim is to be significant at every stage of our working lives. Jean-Pierre Garnier puts it this way: 'Being successful means success in everything. If you look for only one dimension in your life, you'll be sad when it stops and there is nothing else.' We want to be 'happening people'.

I have found the twin-track option to be one of the best ways of dealing with this issue for those in full-time work: one track is a fulfilled working life and the other is a complementary, probably charitable activity. We may be able to use skills honed in the workplace for altruistic purposes or find ways to exploit talents that would otherwise remain unused. I have found it hugely encouraging to have a purpose-led job but also to chair Alpha International, whose vision is to spread the Christian good news. Remembering what God has done for me makes me want to share it with others. However, I do not have the time, skill or calling to be a full-time evangelist. Chairing Alpha International enables me to play a role and share in the excitement. I chose Alpha International, first because I was asked by a close friend, Nicky Gumbel, who pioneered the Alpha course; second because it reflects my own passions; and third because I am able to contribute to its structures and management. I bring a global perspective, experience of fundraising and budgets, and management skills, using my expertise in the workplace to the advantage of a voluntary organization. I usually spend a couple of hours a week on Alpha International, plus the occasional evening dinner and board meeting, phone calls and thinking time at the weekend. This small input of time seems to make a difference. Although I have chosen to work with friends on this, our relationship in this context is professional.

I really enjoy my job working in a busy London hospital as a senior pharmacist. However, I also feel called to prison work. I used to take days off to go on prison visits and to coordinate prayer meetings at my local church for the prisoners whenever I could. I felt increasingly under pressure as I struggled to maintain my commitment to both. I started to consider working a four-day week but felt sure this would not be possible as the department was already short-staffed. To my surprise, my boss agreed to give me Thursdays off. I then discovered that the chaplain at the local prison needed volunteers on a Thursday. This confirmed to me that the decision was right: God was calling me both to pharmacy and to prison work.

(Sarah Stoll, pharmacist)

Hot-desking and job-sharing – new ways of working

The workplace is changing rapidly. Changes range from the desire for smaller networks and supportive teams to new working patterns such as hot-desking, flexi-hours, job-sharing or working from home. These developments will not be problem-free but I hope that they will enable both men and women to enjoy being with their children more while also having a fulfilling career. For couples starting out it is important to discuss the timing of children, particularly in relation to their working patterns over the course of their life together. In some cases, one will be the breadwinner and the other will run the home, whereas others will choose a more flexible working arrangement. Whatever pattern we follow, we need to learn how to take advantage of changes in the workplace to facilitate our callings. One option is portfolio working, where one person takes on several different part-time jobs or roles, thus building up their own unique career portfolio. But we need to take care that these different activities do not lead us into a short-term mentality.

I worked on a charitable project with Nick Turner, who used to have a full-time media consultancy job but left to become a portfolio worker. I asked him for a practical glimpse at his new working week.

For the last three years I have been, so I am reliably informed, a portfolio worker. I have my own media company, run an internet project for a charity, head up the art and media ministry for a church and spend a day a week at art college. This seems to fit the stage of career I am now at and is made possible by structured training and skills development in the past and a belief that anything is possible.

A typical working week consists of fixed days and flexible days – the fixed days are for the jobs or projects that require regular interaction with others and some rigidity of structure. An example of that would be working every Thursday at church – everyone knows I will be there and available, so meetings and work can be booked in regularly. Another fixed day is the day I spend at art college. The flexible days are the days I spend either doing any freelance work for my media company, fitting in my own art studio time or completing the regular but less urgent tasks that are involved with running the internet project.

A typical week looks like this:

Monday –   flexible time, mix of admin, project
             and freelance work
Tuesday –   art studio time (if possible!)

Wednesday –	flexible time, mix of admin, project and freelance work
Thursday –	church
Friday –	art college
Saturday –	hopefully free!
Sunday –	free, though I am sometimes involved in church services

This way of living my life has advantages and disadvantages. On the plus side life is never dull and every day is different. However, I have found that time management is a big issue, particularly when something goes wrong in one part of my portfolio, whether a business deadline, an unfinished painting or an angry email requiring a response. To stop myself going mad I have had to be very disciplined with my time and have also had to make clear to my clients, bosses and colleagues that I will not necessarily be able to respond to all calls and emails immediately (unless urgent). This is probably the biggest pressure I face.

I definitely earn less than when I worked full-time for one organization, because some of my time is spent on my (unpaid) art and charity work. I could not have afforded to work like this in my early years in London and may not always be able to in the future. If we have a family, my wife and I will need to reassess our working patterns and joint income together. I do feel that it has been good for me to step out of the trap of earning as much money as possible, which was incredibly alluring for a while. It is interesting how much money can be saved when you start budgeting without particularly noticing any change in lifestyle!

Even if the mix of jobs and roles seems haphazard to an outsider, I think there needs to be some cohesion to the portfolio. This could be to develop complementary skills, to combine stressful and stress-releasing roles or to fund one part of your life with earnings from another, but the key is to know why you are doing it. I love stressful projects and roles, but only in moderation. I have found painting to be the most stress-releasing activity for me. By enrolling at art college and thus forcing stress-releasing elements into my routine, I have been able to enjoy the stressful times more and also feel more balanced as a person.

My main aim at the moment is to explore areas of my gifts, skills and personality that I had probably repressed for a number of years – especially fine art and creativity in general. As to how this will develop

– I haven't really got a clue, but I want to be open to where God leads me.

(Nick Turner, portfolio worker)

The pressures of modern living, the demands of the workplace, the stress of travel and the many other personal and financial issues we face each day require us to take seriously a comprehensive review of our lifestyle. We are simply not wired by the Maker to work at full tilt without regard to the enduring priorities of our relationships outside the workplace. Of course, it is true to say that certain jobs are more demanding and require greater levels of stress tolerance than others. And we may well have to say, 'It's too hot for me in this kitchen. I'm getting out.' Where we do stay we have to ensure that our priorities reflect God's priorities for our lives. If we weight the scales with our own agenda for achievement we will never live the hard-working, balanced and fulfilled lives for which we were made. God is not honoured by any way of life which dehumanizes us.

Stress

Two hundred men were monitored over ten years for the Work Site Blood Pressure Study, published in the *American Journal of Epidemiology*. The study revealed that stress at work puts the same strain on the heart as being 40 pounds overweight, and that prolonged bouts of tension have the same effect on blood pressure as ageing 30 years.

Of all the lifestyle issues we face today in the workplace, stress is the most prevalent. It is also a national health problem. One in five visits to British doctors by both adults and children is due to stress-related illness. Is it possible to live well in a stressed-out workplace? Is this stress just a fact of modern living? Should we tough it out for as long as possible and then quit? Does faith make a difference?

Hard pressed and hemmed in – what does stress feel like?

We are often tempted to react against the pressure in our lives. In a recent article, the author lamented our stressed lives and offered an unusual, if unreal, solution.

> One of the more distracting things about capitalist culture . . . is that there is no stupor, no time to vegetate. What I would suggest is more time wasting, less stimulation. We need time to lie fallow like we did in childhood, so we can recuperate. Rather than be constantly told what you want and be pressurized to go after it, I think we would benefit greatly from spells of vaguely restless boredom in which desire can crystallize.

We all know what it feels like to be stressed. It is the point at which others' expectations of us and our ability to deliver fail to match. All around us every day we hear, 'I'm stressed out', 'I'm really pushed', 'I'm out of control', 'I'm not coping'. Exhaustion and stress go hand in hand. St Paul, writing to the Corinthians, uses the image of being 'hard pressed on every side' (2 Corinthians 4:8), or, put another way, being squeezed from every side. I know that feeling as part of everyday life: being squeezed like toothpaste through the tube. There are too many demands and not enough time. There's no space to stop and think.

Jesus tells the story of the sower who plants his seed: some of it falls on stony ground, some falls among the thorns and some in good soil. The seed – the teaching of God – that falls in good soil germinates and produces fruit. I am particularly struck by the image of the seed that falls among thorns, because this is so often what happens to the Christian at work. Here the words are heard and a new lifestyle is adopted, 'but the worries of this life, the deceitfulness of wealth and the desires for other things come in and choke the word, making it unfruitful' (Mark 4:19). The word Jesus uses for 'choke' is a very powerful one. It is not merely describing a coughing fit, but a totally overwhelming choking, almost a drowning experience. We can be overwhelmed in many ways; by the big questions – Why am I here? What am I working for? We can be deceived by the promises of material wealth. Or we can simply be stressed by the other things: long hours, unrealistic deadlines, targets, appraisals, paying the mortgage, filling the fridge, keeping up.

At times, stress manifests itself physically: not being able to eat, stomach problems, insomnia or tightness around the chest. It may also show itself psychologically: we are distracted and unable to concentrate on our work, beset by irrational fears or aggressive to our colleagues. Stress is also spiritual. Above everything else, I have found that it destroys perspective, often making me become self-absorbed. Stress strangles our relationships both with other people and with God because we cannot lift our heads to see the wider picture. This preoccupation easily becomes obsessive and we lose the ability to think beyond our current fixation. As the parable shows, stress chokes us into low productivity at work.

I normally have the good fortune to sleep extremely well and have even been known to nod off at the dinner table. If, therefore, I wake preoccupied in the middle of the night, I know that I must be deeply stressed. On one occasion, I was involved with a major securities transaction. Investment banks buy and sell shares as part of their day-to-day business. Often sellers of shares want a fixed price for their shares and invite a bank to purchase these shares before offering them for sale to investors. The risk is then passed to the bank and the seller has certainty of the proceeds. Until the bank is able to dispose of the shares it is on the hook. If the price goes up money is made and if it goes down losses are incurred. We had just made a very difficult pricing decision, and I was anxious to see whether the market would prove us right the following morning. I woke in the early hours, tossed and turned but could not get back to sleep. The critical day had not started so all I could do was wait. I could not even talk to anyone as it was the middle of the night. Restless anxiety continued to eat away at me. I decided to get up and somewhat mechanically read through some Psalms to try to obtain a wider perspective. I prayed that our judgement would be vindicated.

The next morning, however, the share price declined. My anxiety thus continued for a few days until, happily in this case, the price recovered and we could sell the shares without loss. This does not always happen. There are times for all of us when we simply have to sweat it out, knowing that God is with us through stressful times even if we don't always get the result we hope for.

Stress is not necessarily the same as pressure. Many of us thrive under pressure but wilt under persistent stress.

Pressure comes from without – and I do not mind pressure. In many ways it gives me a buzz. I would define pressure as being challenged by a project or situation, whether in terms of complexity or timescale or both. I find that it stimulates me and makes the adrenalin flow so that I can accomplish more than seems possible. Stress, which I do not relish, comes from within. To me, stress is the pressure I put on myself internally to meet unrealistic deadlines. This leads to frustration or even a sense of hopelessness about the enormity of the task. I find this very disempowering. While pressure stimulates, stress drains and grinds down, and yet is worn by some colleagues as a badge of honour.

(Hannah Reid, City lawyer)

Jesus and stress – a way through

Stress is not a modern invention, although its intensity may have increased in our generation. Jesus was no stranger to stress. He knew what it was like to feel hemmed in, but he also knew that he was called to a wider purpose – to see goodness prevail over evil. He was in constant demand as a public figure – a celebrity: people wanted him to be king, and to be available to the crowds. He knew exhaustion and the need to get away. He confronted the merchants in the temple and drove them out when their actions desecrated the place of worship. He was misunderstood even by his own disciples, denied by his friend Peter and betrayed by Judas.

If I am very pushed and exhausted after travelling a lot, I often draw strength from one stressful day in the life of Jesus recorded in Luke 8:22–56. Jesus and the disciples set out in a boat. He falls asleep, I believe exhausted, so that even a raging storm does not wake him up. He is woken by panicking disciples and he quells the storm. On setting foot on the opposite shore he exorcizes a demon-possessed man, bringing ruin to the local Gadarene farmer whose herd of pigs crash into the lake. After that, the fearful people ask him to leave them. Hardly has he returned across the lake than he accedes to Jairus' plea to visit his dying daughter. En route he is mobbed and his garment touched in faith by a woman with bleeding, whom he heals.

Then Jairus' daughter dies. He is told not to bother but Jesus nonetheless presses on. He arrives and shuts up the funeral wailers, saying that she is asleep and not dead. They laugh at him but he raises her from the dead. It is all here: exhaustion, loneliness, travelling and trying to catch up on sleep, interrupted sleep, the demands of friends, the fear of failure, the taunts of the worldly wise.

When Jesus preached his first sermon in Nazareth, his home town rejoiced at his remarkable teaching – he was the local boy made good. Luke tells us that 'all spoke well of him' (Luke 4:22). But then, within the day, the temperature changed as he preached: 'All the people in the synagogue were furious when they heard this. They got up, drove him out of the town, and took him to the brow of the hill on which the town was built, in order to throw him down the cliff. But he walked right through the crowd and went on his way' (Luke 4:28–30). This is a great example for us. When it seemed that everyone had turned against him, Jesus did not run for cover; he walked through the midst of the crowd and went on his way. This is the authority of a person convinced of his calling and of the power of God to help him. Jesus said, 'I know where I came from and where I am going' (John 8:14).

We can do what Jesus did. Many times I have turned to this teaching when I have felt the world closing in on me. When we feel overwhelmed by the demands of the workplace, we don't have to outflank the pressure around us. We can, and we must, face it head on. The Spirit of God empowers us, like Christ, to walk through the midst of our stress.

Chilled not choked – how do we deal with stress?

Some stress, for example that which results in clinical depression, requires medical attention. However, my aim here is to consider stress in everyday work situations.

When Jesus comforts his disciples shortly before his death, he starts with the perspective of eternity: 'In my Father's house are many rooms; if it were not so, I would have told you. I am going there to prepare a place for you. And if I go and prepare a place for you, I will come back and take you to be with me' (John 14:2–3a). When we see our lives in the security of this wider context, the things that stress us out can seem much more manageable. Jesus goes on to speak about the promised Holy Spirit and says,

'Peace I leave with you; my peace I give you. I do not give to you as the world gives. Do not let your hearts be troubled and do not be afraid' (John 14:27). We need to root our lives in the peace that Christ has given us if we are to deal effectively with stress. This means nurturing our relationship with God at all times through consistent reading of the Bible, developing intimacy with God, prayer and the use of other spiritual disciplines.

In Psalm 18, David says, 'In my distress [i.e. 'When I was under pressure'] I called to the Lord; I cried to my God for help' (Psalm 18:6). This call is answered in verse 19: 'He brought me out into a spacious place; he rescued me because he delighted in me.' These verses have meant more to me in the harshness of the working environment than almost any other Psalm. The love of God – his delight in me – transforms my perspective in the workplace. The 'spacious place' of verse 19 is what I long for – room to manoeuvre and a chance to recover God's peace. God is the space giver; the devil is the space invader. I therefore try to look for the God-given spacious place in the midst of stress. Christian stress-busting is not a new self-help technique but an outworking of following Christ. I have tried to follow seven biblical strategies to keep stress in check. I hope they may be helpful to you.

1. Stay healthy

At its most basic, we need to look after our bodies by taking regular breaks, eating well and exercising regularly. Our bodies are, after all, temples of the Holy Spirit (1 Corinthians 6:19) and need to be looked after. This is simply common sense, but in times of stress, it can be the first thing to go. I remember a time in the middle of a very complicated take-over bid by one major UK company of another, when I tried to take a break each day to go to a nearby gym. I could not plan ahead but grabbed the opportunity whenever it arose. This partly helped to clear my mind, but mostly it relieved the tension of constant decision-making. A lawyer told me that during one seemingly never-ending deal, he often found himself at ten at night checking whether the team had consumed anything other than caffeine that day. Generally they hadn't and he ordered in food for them. He was amazed how much quicker they got through everything once they had eaten!

2. Fight fear

I remember reading Psalm 112:7 one morning to learn that the people who trust the Lord 'will have no fear of bad news; their hearts are steadfast, trusting in the Lord'. While I was praying I sensed that all was not well at work and that it would be an important day. I had no idea what that meant, but I knew that the Spirit of God was preparing me. The words 'will have no fear of bad news' went through my head throughout the day. At the end of the day I was called into the chairman's office. He told me that one of my best clients had decided that I was not the right person to advise him. In normal circumstances I would have been devastated. Of course I felt gutted, but the day's preparation meant that I was ready to receive the news. I did not need to fear bad news. This did not mean that there wasn't any, but that I did not need to fear it. This assurance enabled me to come through a difficult time with confidence. The client wrote me a very gracious letter explaining his reasons; I knew that he was right. I spoke to him and was able to accept his judgement without rancour. I did not feel the need to re-run history or to justify my actions, which would have been my natural reaction. I then felt a curious freedom in handing over the account to a colleague. I was able to offer help behind the scenes with genuine willingness. I had, after all, received the tip-off!

3. Take joy seriously

In 1 Thessalonians, Paul writes, 'Be joyful always' (5:16). In times of stress we particularly need to look around us and focus consciously on what lifts our spirits. When streaming out of the crowded Underground station, or stuck in traffic, take time to notice a bird in a tree or a beautiful piece of architecture. I remember rushing out of a meeting and seeing an elderly couple holding hands and chatting as they walked down the street together. This boosted my day, reminding me of enduring values beyond the day-to-day stress. Small things can make a big difference to our mood. It is valuable to build up a reservoir of the specific ways in which God has helped us in the past to remind us that God is real and that he is good.

4. *Take an emotional break*

None of us functions well in prolonged periods of unremitting stress. If I feel I am losing my sense of perspective, I often make a phone call to a friend or send an email which has nothing to do with work. I find it restores my sense of humanity to connect with people in different situations from my own. Even if they are also stressed, just talking together takes me out of the cocoon of my own preoccupations.

In times of stress, my wife Fi and I have to work out what is the best way of spending time together. If I am particularly tired, a dinner for two can become an action replay of my stressful day. If both of us are under pressure the temptation can be to compete about how bad things have been. A trip to the theatre or cinema can enable us to enjoy being together without increasing our stress levels. Sometimes it helps, if both of us agree, not to talk about a particularly pressing issue but instead to try to enjoy simply being together.

In times of high stress, I often feel desperate for a time of sung worship. I long for the times of worship on Sunday, or try to meet with a few others to worship. Worshipping together helps me to maintain the intimacy of my relationship with God, which stress can so easily erode.

5. Minister in the opposite spirit

Paul says, 'We work hard with our own hands. When we are cursed, we bless; when we are persecuted, we endure it; when we are slandered, we answer kindly' (1 Corinthians 4:12–13). When a colleague trashes our work, we shouldn't snap back but instead commend them on a piece of their work. And when others criticize us, we should aim to answer gently. This is easy to agree with but very hard to do. I try and change gears by asking for help from the Spirit of God – and only then do I speak. This is the spiritual equivalent of counting to ten. But so often I fail – and lash out. I then feel dreadful. Ministering in the opposite spirit is usually a painful process.

After only a few days in my new job at the hospital, I seemed to keep having altercations with one of the reception staff. She would respond to my polite civilities with what appeared to be complaint after complaint. She would claim that my handwriting wasn't clear enough (this from a woman who works with doctors!) and object to my clinic list being handed in a few minutes late. I assumed that it was because I was a lowly physiotherapist and not a terribly grand consultant that she treated me with such disdain.

Several weeks later I had to cancel a clinic at short notice and so left word with the reception staff. When I returned there was a barrage of complaints from patients who had travelled to the hospital before being informed that the clinic was cancelled. These complaints finally gave me the impetus I needed to confront the issues. Despite a creeping feeling that I was being bullied by someone in a less senior position, I chose a quiet moment and sat down with the receptionist. I decided not to pull rank but rather to ask whether I had offended her and why she hadn't cancelled my patients. After the inevitable momentary defensiveness it turned out she had assumed that I had my own secretarial support and that the clinic patients were my sole responsibility. Our mistaken assumptions about each other's roles and attitudes proved to be the only stumbling block to working out a solution.

Several months later, she took the time to come to me and, much to her credit, apologised. On reflection

I was so pleased that I had not reacted in a
retaliatory manner as this would have compounded
the difficulties of both our situations.

(Anita Patel, physiotherapist)

6. *Take control of our thoughts*

In my experience, in times of high anxiety the prevailing
wind is negativity and thoughts can easily spiral down-
wards. A persistent questioning can arise from the depths
of the inner self relating to fear of the future, what others
think of us or whether there is any significance in what we
are doing. When this happens, the first thing I try to do is
to reject the thoughts that are without substance. I then
remind myself of one of the many attributes of God – for
example his love – and then dwell on it. Paul wrote, 'whatever is true, whatever is noble, whatever is right, whatever
is pure, whatever is lovely, whatever is admirable – if
anything is excellent or praiseworthy – think about such
things' (Philippians 4:8). The mind is a gateway which we
control. With God's help we can choose to open it to good
and close it to fear, uncertainty and self-righteousness. In
Paradise Lost, Milton captures this thought: 'The mind is
its own place, and in itself can make a Heav'n of Hell, a
Hell of Heaven.' It is within our control to regulate what
we dwell on: the discipline of breaking a negative spiral is a
key weapon in our desire to eliminate stress.

One way of breaking the drag of negative thoughts is to go on a 'starvation diet'. Set a time – say, a day – and deliberately try to starve yourself of any negative thoughts. At the same time allow space for the Spirit of God to engage your mind with the good, the wholesome and the positive aspects of life and meditate on these.

A business development manager told me that in times of stress he tries to find a quiet place and speak his concerns aloud. He also keeps a pad of paper next to his bed to write down thoughts that preoccupy him and prevent him from sleeping. These techniques stop his anxieties from dominating his thought-life and leave him free to move on.

Different strategies work for different people. Steve, a print worker, found it helpful to set aside a 'worry time'. He told me that while running his business he went through a terrible experience and was frantic with anxiety about a certain issue. A friend advised him to set aside a time of day to worry about it, for example fifteen minutes between 9am and 9.15am. This technique helped keep him sane. If a letter or fax came through about the issue, he would just put it in the in-tray and read it in his 'worry time'. If there was a phone call, he said that he was busy and arranged to call back in the worry time! If he woke up in the middle of the night in a panic, he would say to himself, 'No, I am not thinking about this now. I will think about it tomorrow at 9am.' He found that when he did this, it shrunk the problem and made it manageable. Life could carry on outside the worry time, and it stopped him being anxious all the time and having endless circular conversations with his wife.

I have also found it helpful to break time into manageable sections, sometimes aiming just to get through the morning until lunchtime. It is important to set a future point to look forward to, for example, deciding to watch Manchester United next Wednesday. This can help counter the feeling that there is no end in sight. When huge problems seem to be hovering on the horizon, I try to remember Jesus' words: 'Therefore do not worry about tomorrow, for tomorrow will worry about itself. Each day has enough trouble of its own' (Matthew 6:34). When stress is high we should live in a world of contracting horizons.

7. Pray and read the Bible

For me, the most important way to gain perspective in times of stress is through prayer, remembering of course that the primary objective of prayer is to bring glory to God, and not to beat stress. Paul says in Philippians, 'Do not be anxious about anything, but in everything, by prayer and petition, with thanksgiving, present your requests to God' (4:6). I know of very tense meetings that I have attended when parties have been at loggerheads with each other. I try to turn to God and to pray silently. The acrimony often, but by no means invariably, seems to disappear. I cannot prove the causality, but it seems to happen more often the more I pray.

Intercession on the run is not sufficient but can be helpful. Most of my petitionary prayer happens when I am travelling. I know many people who pray whenever going to a fixed point in the office – the lift, the coffee machine or photocopier. We also need to set patterns of prayer. Monday morning is a good time to prepare spiritually for the week ahead. As the week starts, I like to remind myself that there is a spiritual 'can-do' aspect to work, however stressful the week may turn out to be. I think of Numbers 13:30, where Caleb said, 'We should go up and take possession of the land, for we can certainly do it.' On weekday mornings I try to pray and read at least the New Testament section of my Bible (divided into 365 daily readings from the Old and New Testaments) before I get to work. I consider the weekends 'catch-up time', a chance to build up spiritual capital, which can run down very fast during the week.

I was very struck by the testimony of the power of prayer recounted by a former colleague of mine who left to set up his own business.

I miscalculated quite severely how long it would take to get a consulting business of this kind to break even. Like most entrepreneurs, I had taken out a mortgage on the house to provide us with enough money to live for eighteen months while we got it going. I had neglected to foresee the swift and dramatic business downturn of 2001–02. So we were left with cash resources dwindling and not much in the way of business prospects. During this period, I started feeling massively stressed, upset and on the verge of tears on a regular basis. I had never before been without money, and it was a very unfamiliar experience. My wife and I had cut back expenses pretty hard, but we were still spending more than I was able to earn. I felt embarrassed talking to my friends, who would inevitably ask how it was going. I tried to be cheerful, but it was inauthentic.

I started praying like never before, reading the Bible each morning at 6:00 or 6:30, the overall structure provided by the Lord's Prayer. I did not ask for too much in the way of money, but rather that I would be filled with peace, and would do the kind of work God wanted me to do. I began to pray for guidance, wisdom and discernment. I also started praying a lot for others, the church and friends, and attempted to be thankful for what I had. Sometimes an hour would go by and I wouldn't even notice.

The effect of this praying was quite amazing. When I was really going through the stressful patch, I would not stop praying until I felt filled with the Spirit. I don't know how to define that except to say I felt confident and relaxed during each day that things were going to turn out ok. Here I was, an entrepreneur running out of money, in the middle of a terrible recession, realizing that he does not really have a clue what he is doing or what his product is, and yet feeling quite relaxed about it. People started telling me how well I looked, younger and healthier. I could not get over this at all. I can honestly say I went through the hardest time of my life profession-ally, and felt younger at the end of it!

I also started to develop real compassion for people who have to struggle with money every month, and I could see how debilitating money wor-ries can be, especially if one has a family to provide for. It has been a very humbling experience for a former arrogant and successful banker. God taught me a valuable lesson. I determined that when the money started flowing, we would give away what we did not need, rather than hoarding it for a 'rainy day' or for 'financial independence'. It has really changed

my values. I would not have traded this experience
for the world.

(Miles Protter, Managing Partner of
The Values Partnership)

Prayer is the vital oxygen for living. It is simply not possible to function without these regular times of hearing and
then recalibrating our ways accordingly. We need to understand our own temperament and then to find a prayer
routine that suits us, including Bible reading, reflecting,
singing and meditating. Eugene Peterson, the writer and
Bible translator, talks of the Bible as 'everyday robust
sanity'. We need this reality check, which comes from reading the Bible, to de-stress our lives. The most liberating
moment comes when we realize that there is no one-size-
fits-all prayer methodology. We all need to pray but the
way in which we do so should reflect the rich variety of
God's ways of speaking to us. One way I find most powerful is the prayer of praise. Praise is our weapon of first
resort. We can live under pressure if our perspective of
God is right. Our understanding of the greatness of God
leads us to despair of our own strength and to turn to
God, the only one who can make sense of the complex
world he has created. Praise is the war cry of the Christian
asserting God's supremacy over the whole of life including the workplace. I believe that nothing breaks the

self-centredness of a centred life as much as the words, 'I praise you Lord'.

During the Battle of Trafalgar 200th anniversary cele-brations in 2005, I became fascinated by the life of Nelson. Twice daily, all his life, he studied and recorded the weather – what the wind, waves, swell and temperature were doing. He did so whether on land or on sea. It must have been the most dull routine! Yet, in the moment of critical judgement at the Battle of Trafalgar, Nelson drew on this reservoir of knowledge and insight as he observed that a change in the swell of the sea pointed to an advanc-ing storm days before it broke. Instead of having a conven-tional battle where the two lines of ships lined up against each other in parallel, he seized the advantage offered by the sea to slice through and destroy the combined armada. His daily habit gave him the experience and confidence to make that decisive judgement at a critical time in this nation's history.

We never know when the storms of life will hit us. We therefore need to build up our memory bank and to be prepared. One way of doing so is to develop the daily habit of regular prayer. We will then be in much better shape to face the unexpected stress when it comes.

Failure, Disappointment and Hope

Everyone experiences failure and disappointment. It often starts early in life and the memories, very often trivial, stay with us, and sometimes shape our decisions even decades later. When I was about sixteen, I was chairman of the school debating society. A major debate about the apartheid system was organized, and I prepared myself to speak passionately against it. I felt that the righteousness of our cause would easily win. However, we lost. I realized that I had not taken into account the forces of naked prejudice. This failure to persuade a group of my peers of such obvious injustice has never left me, and even now I prefer not to think about the pain of what seemed to me a deeply personal rejection. Objectively, it was a passing moment of little consequence, but it has stayed with me. In our working lives it is unusual not to experience disappointment. We are overlooked for promotion or made redundant; a crucial deal folds or we fail to secure an agent; a team member betrays us or lets us down, or we make a mistake that fills us with shame. And what is shame but that which, when recalled to our conscious mind, we wish were not there? In these situations, how is it possible to find hope, deal with failure and disappointment and to find a spur to drive us on beyond the gloom?

Faith and eternity – the basis of Christian hope

In difficult times, I have often tried to learn from Paul's example. He knows where the source of his strength comes from: 'To this end I labour, struggling with all [God's] energy, which so powerfully works in me' (Colossians 1:29). The energy for living well comes from a source outside of us yet works to change us from within. The source of Christian hope arises from the knowledge that we are made by a God who loves each one of us. We have renewed a relationship with him through the life, death and resurrection of Jesus. We look forward to his return. It is this cosmic context that provides the framework for our everyday lives. In a fast moving world I think it is essential that we fix our minds and our hearts on the hope that Christ has given us, and move the other pieces around this.

Christian hope is not mere optimism nor a projection of our desires. It is not the same as saying, 'I hope it doesn't rain.' Paul writes that 'hope does not disappoint us, because God has poured out his love into our hearts by the Holy Spirit, whom he has given us' (Romans 5:5). Jesus inaugurated the kingdom of God when he came to earth, and he won the decisive victory over evil and disappointment on the cross. As we work in partnership with God, drawing his values into the world, we are called to lay down our lives, identifying with Jesus on the cross and sharing in the same resurrection power. Paul uses rich commercial words to describe this relationship. He writes: '. . . he anointed us, set his seal of ownership on us, and put his spirit in our hearts as a deposit, guaranteeing what is to come' (2 Corinthians 1:21–22). Anointing is the word used for 'investing in'. God has invested in our lives, marking us with an outward sign (seal) of his ownership. The Holy Spirit is a 'deposit' guaranteeing now the full payment later. Thus we are utterly secure in this life because Christ has underwritten his investment in us. Our lives therefore have eternal value.

I remember my student days in South Africa, at a very dark time in its history. We used to crouch over the radio, listening to the BBC World Service. We were passionate about abolishing apartheid and establishing justice, and it gave us such hope for our own work to hear from the regular broadcasts that there was another world where people lived by decent values. We all need some experience outside ourselves to cling to when our hope is under pressure.

The Christian is sustained by the knowledge that this world is not all that there is.

The great exchange – how do we deal with our mistakes?

Dominating the City of London is a magnificent building called the Royal Exchange, where major commercial trans-actions were carried out. As I walked past the building one morning, I suddenly saw in my mind's eye an image of what Christ did on the cross for us. It was a royal exchange. Exchange is the image of the market place. Financial traders talk about convertible bonds and interest rate swaps, and all of us have paged through *Exchange and Mart* and understand the concept of bartering goods. Every day we can ask God to take our guilt, mistakes and failures and exchange them for peace, security and pur-pose. We enter into the trade simply by asking him to take the acts and omissions which cause displeasure to him – our sin. This is as real a transaction as anyone buying, for example, a car: you take your money, you give it to the dealer, and he exchanges it for a vehicle. But there is a difference. We bring nothing. Jesus gives us a trade that we do not deserve, and completes the bargain as if he were on both sides.

In 2002 what was previously legal tender in Europe –

for example the French franc, the deutschemark, and the peseta – was converted into a new currency, the euro. It is now not possible to spend a French franc in a shop. Only the euro is acceptable. Imagine in a few years' time someone going into a *bureau de change* with a stack of French francs and asking for euros. He would of course be rejected, because he brings nothing to the trade. The French francs cannot earn him a euro – they are worthless. Imagine if someone were prepared to accept the trade. We would think them either astonishingly stupid or amazingly generous. Why would someone exchange valuable assets for worthless ones? But this is of course precisely what Jesus did on the cross. He entered into the Great Exchange, by which he gave us his riches for our poverty. 'For you know the grace of our Lord Jesus Christ, that though he was rich, yet for your sakes he became poor, so that you through his poverty might become rich' (2 Corinthians 8:9). This is a compelling verse: riches for poverty; life for death; freedom for guilt.

Ongoing forgiveness – how can we restore relationships?

To maintain good relationships, we need to learn to say sorry and to practise forgiveness in the workplace. You may say forgiveness is fine at church, but surely not at work.

But as Christians, we know that we are forgiven sinners, and this enables us to take the lead. I find that when I have been working under demanding conditions, particularly if I am overly tired, I need to be especially vigilant about my reactions to people.

Whenever we feel that we have stepped out of line, I think we need to apologize. Similarly, if we feel we have been wronged, it is constructive to approach the other person only after a short interval (perhaps 24/48 hours), to allow our feelings to cool down. We need to work towards an attitude of grace, taking minor issues in our stride.

> I work for rather difficult characters – brilliant in their way but not gifted in managing people. I can find myself building up a list of resentments against them. I have to stop myself and make the effort to pray for them, however little I feel like it, and forgive them for the irritations and injustices I feel I have had to put up with. This always helps me to see them as real people with their own pressures, and improves the working relationship.
>
> (Ian Lloyd, solicitor)

One of the great difficulties in the world today is truth decay – many treat truth as a tradable commodity, only buying into it if the return looks promising. It is not just that we should be able to trust particular individuals to tell the truth, but that trustworthy behaviour should start to infuse organizations, so that integrity is once again seen as a value to aspire to. Without trust and integrity the free market is endangered. When I attended a recent World Economic Forum in Davos, Switzerland, 'Tough Trust' was the topic for discussion. I thought it was an arresting title. It is tough to rely on others but we need to do so. We need each other, however much we prefer to go it alone. This trusting interdependence is drawn from the Trinity. God is reflected in these endeavours precisely because this is what happens in the eternal Godhead. Could there be a greater model of tough trust than Jesus working with his disciples in a trusting relationship, with all the well-documented strain and joy that this entailed?

But how, practically, do we build trust again once it has been fractured? All of us have deep memories of broken relationships at work. Your idea is taken by someone and passed off as his or her own; someone lies to you about your performance at work; or you are let down without excuse at the last moment on a crucial project. At some time or another we say to ourselves – or to others – 'I can't trust Nicola or John again.' Yet we know in reality that we have to work together.

On one occasion, a colleague was not straight with me, and I subsequently found out from others about his bad-mouthing me. I was furious. Half of me wanted nothing more to do with him; half of me knew that we had to work together under one roof and therefore we had to talk. To be honest, I never wanted to trust him again. But we are created in God's image. The certainties and ferocity of self-righteous outpourings when we are hurt bend to the persistent but much more tentative proddings of conscience. In these circumstances we should take the first step, even if we do so gingerly. After all, it's a very raw nerve that is touched. There is nothing wrong with being wary – but wariness should not replace the willingness to build a new relationship. Reconciliation is at the heart of faith and this pushes us, usually against our natural instincts, to begin to rebuild trust. And God who is trustworthy teaches us to trust again.

But how do we start to put things right? Step one is the desire to set matters straight. Here too we know that God inclines our hearts towards reconciliation, so that even if we do not feel inclined to make peace we can ask him to give us the grace to do so. Thereafter an approach needs to be made. In my case this was a short handwritten letter – email is too often the vehicle for quick rage. Then there should be a frank discussion. There is no lasting value in not being up front about the facts. Expect a response – even a vigorous one. After all, the accusations that one makes regarding a break in trust go to the essence of any person's self-esteem. After the meeting there is not an automatic re-set to the status quo ante. That takes time, but our behaviour has to reflect the reality that we have totally forgiven that person. I hope that I did so and that he knew that no grudges were kept.

The 'Our Father' is invaluable for this reason: 'Forgive us our shortfalls as we forgive those who have wronged us.' We forgive as we have been forgiven. We say this prayer not nearly enough. It is truly the manifesto of the person at work. Thus invoked, an energy that comes from outside our own being enables us to walk in the freedom of new trust. Yes, there will be an accusation of naivety. 'Don't trust others' is after all a slogan for many who have been hurt at work. Sometimes we have to live with the consequences of trusting too readily. That could be part of our calling to suffer with Christ.

Jesus longed for the trust of those around him. He took the risk of trusting his disciples. All trust involves risk. He was badly let down and betrayed. Yet forgiveness and restoration lay at the heart of his message. The drive to trust again arises not out of the need of the workplace but from the very nature of God. Every fractured trust impairs our humanity. Every forgiven breach strengthens it. That's God's way in the world.

Failure and disappointment – an opportunity to grow

It is inevitable that some projects we are involved in will fail, but it is not true that you or I are failures. I remember a young banker telling me, 'I am a failure.' This is a devastating statement, which may have deadly psychological consequences. It is more accurate to say, 'I have failed in this project.' This enables us to face the reality of the situation without condemning our whole life and person to failure.

Then we need to deal with the chain of negative emotions that can be set off by a perceived failure. Failure is like a train that pulls behind it a coach of disappointment, and linked to that a coach of self-pity, and then a coach of rejection, then another coach of 'I've had enough', and finally a coach of all-pervading pessimism. I try not to let my sense of disappointment about a particular failure spread to other areas of my life. I remember working intensely for several months putting together a takeover bid, which was rejected. I was left with an empty diary and no adrenalin, wondering what could have been done better. I went home feeling low and lacking the resilience to cope with minor irritations. On these occasions, I find that what helps me most is to remind myself that God is so much bigger than an adverse decision or a failed transaction. Reading the Psalms aloud and alone brings a perspective of the greatness and power of God. Restoring our perspective keeps our feelings of disappointment in their proper place. We are only failures if Christ fails in us – and that he will never do. We can be confident that he who began a good work in us will carry it through to completion (Philippians 1:6).

In our achievement-orientated culture, we tend to feel ashamed of our failures. We view them as wholly negative and try to cover them up. But the way we grow is not by pretending that all is well, but by facing disappointment head on, acknowledging the facts. When the disciples had been working all night and were asked whether they had caught any fish, they must have been tempted to justify their failure. Instead they said, 'We have no fish.' But they still believed in Jesus' ability to turn their situation around. When they followed his instruction to fish on the right side, their nets were filled to bursting (John 21:6). Similarly, we need to be brutally honest about our failures and to be open to God's guidance, especially in times of crushing disappointment. Constructive criticism helps us to learn from our mistakes and is one of the main ways in which we can improve and grow. As a young trainee I was working on the first privatization issue for the government, the sale of BP shares. I had to prepare a crucial share exchange document, which would enable the shares to be distributed from the government to millions of new investors. I messed it up. There was a group of people around my desk waiting. Stress was high and a deadline was approaching. The chairman of the bank was also there and was quite entitled to go ballistic. Instead, he gave the others a new task and when alone with me ticked me off (quite rightly) and then showed me how to sort out the vital document. That day I learnt a lot about share exchanges, but perhaps more about learning from mistakes.

Failures help to kill our pride and develop humility. This is crucial if we want to follow Jesus and develop a godly character. God promises to work in all things for the good of those who love him (Romans 8:28). This does not mean that he inflicts failure on us, but it does mean that he can use it. He brings good out of bad situations in the most unexpected ways – even when we can't possibly imagine how this might happen. This is illustrated in the life of Joseph, who was sold by his brothers, abused, imprisoned, but was finally reinstated as the first and only Israeli to become Prime Minister of Egypt. 'You intended to harm me, but God intended it for good' (Genesis 50:20).

We went through a three-year period where virtually everything seemed to be going wrong. I lost my job and as a result we got behind on our mortgage repayments. We made a conscious decision not to hide our situation from those who asked, even when they expected a cheery 'Christian' answer. At times we felt very vulnerable, particularly when God seemed absent. We realized that we had always assumed that things would work out more or less as we wanted in the end. We have learnt to loosen our grip on the future, and on good days feel excitement about where God might lead us. We also live more fully in the present and generally worry less. We have also noticed that our openness about what we've been going through seems to have helped other people to be honest with us about their own hidden struggles, leading to a new depth of relationship.

(Roger Philip, self-employed)

Recovering from disappointment – five steps to renew our hope

Laurence van der Post, the South African philosopher and anthropologist who spent his life observing the social patterns of contemporary society and of the nomadic San people in South Africa, remarked, 'the lesson of history for me is that men and their societies can endure and surmount any enormities except a state of meaninglessness' (*Walk with the Bushmen*).

Living each day at work with hope and purpose is essential for our well-being. It is true that those who are purpose-led have a positive outlook on life and produce better results both at work and outside it, influencing the communities in which they live. So it is important to recover hope when, through failure and disappointment, we have lost its power to keep us expectant. How do we do it? Here are five pointers that I have found helpful when trying to recover from disappointment.

1. Turn to God

Following Jesus' crucifixion, two of the disciples were walking to Emmaus, a village about seven miles from Jerusalem. As they discussed recent events, somebody came and joined them, and finding them downcast, enquired what they were talking about. It was only later that they realized the man was Jesus. Initially they were so preoccupied with their disappointment that they failed to recognize that the Lord of hope was walking alongside them. It is important to face our disappointments honestly and to acknowledge how they make us feel. However, if we do not keep disappointment in its place, it can overwhelm us, and we too risk forgetting that the Lord of hope walks with us through good and bad, and has promised never to abandon us (Matthew 28:20).

When we are down, we often instinctively want to turn

away from God, in some way implicating him in our misfortune. This is a great mistake. If we follow the self-help theories, we will dig inside ourselves only to find that there is nothing there to pick us up. We need to take the initiative to lift our heads towards God. As we do so, we are reminded of his love for us, his victory on the cross and the power of the resurrection.

There is a 'tensed waiting' on earth as we live in the hope created by the resurrection, which has not yet been fulfilled. Not only is work imperfect but creation as a whole groans in imperfection, waiting for the new heaven and the new earth promised by God. The hope of Christ's return enables us to live expectantly even if our present circumstances at work are harsh and negative.

2. Face the facts

Realism is vital when we come to deal with our disappointments. I find enormous encouragement from the description in Romans of Abraham who, we are told, 'Without weakening in his faith, faced the fact that his body was as good as dead – since he was about 100 years old – and that Sarah's womb was also dead. Yet he did not waver through unbelief regarding the promise of God' (Romans 4:19–20). He faced the facts that they were both past childbearing age, yet remained open to God's power to give them a child.

The facts are a radical reality. We need to avoid fantasies and daydreams of what might have been when we deal with our own discouragements: there is no value in an indulgent reconstruction of the past. It is God alone who can change our situation, enabling us to stop dwelling in the past so that he can transform and empower our future.

3. Meditate on Scripture

Led by the Spirit, we find a promise of God in the Bible appropriate to our situation. We then read it, mull it over and say it aloud until we digest its meaning and its truth becomes part of our being. I find it helpful to memorize and meditate upon particular verses, because hope is so often attacked by negativity and fear. I have committed to memory Romans 15:13, 'May the God of hope fill you with all joy and peace as you trust in him, so that you may overflow with hope by the power of the Holy Spirit.' By his creative Holy Spirit, God enables us to grow in hope, breaking the bounds of our own narrowness and transforming areas of our lives that we have constructed in the belief that God cannot really make a difference.

4. Keep a journal

I normally find it easier to talk than to write, but if I am going through a particularly difficult time, I find it helpful to keep a journal. This enables me to articulate what I am thinking and feeling. Written words seem to have a more objective ring to them – and can also be reviewed at a later date. As I review past disappointments, I can often see God's hand at work, bringing good out of situations that seemed hopeless at the time. In retrospect, I can recognize that God gave me 'eternal encouragement and good hope' (2 Thessalonians 2:16). The focus of my recollection is changed from 'yet another failure' to the good that came out of a time of rejection and disillusionment.

5. *Persevere in hope*

We naturally long for instant gratification and for a sudden change of mood when we are burdened and feeling a loss of hope in our lives. This is seldom what happens. Character is developed by learning to live through disappointment and recovering hope for the long term. We are not promised that at the end of each day there will be a reversal of the weights that have dragged us down. But we are encouraged that if we persevere, God will enable us to keep going when we are ready to pack it all in.

At a recent U2 concert, Bono recalled his father's advice to him as a young man starting out on a career: 'Don't dream. To dream is to be disappointed.' Fortunately, Bono did not take this advice. He dared to dream and he risked disappointment. Even if we face disillusionment when our dreams fade or fail, we can emerge from it because Christian hope is dynamic and powerful, whereas disappointment tends to constrict us, reducing our motivation and contracting our horizons. Christian hope expresses abundance, abandonment, creativity and an openness to renewal.

A client once said to me, 'You can either be a pussy cat or a tiger in this deal. Now go and be a tiger.' Christian hope has too often been domesticated as if it were a pussy cat, a good feeling or a good cause – something to keep us going. We need to recover the tiger – a wild hope.

The unforced rhythms of grace – how to live with hope

When we are down we tend to live dysfunctional lives. It is as if there is a constant sore that we cannot get rid of, which reminds us of the negative tow in our lives. The disciples were often brought down, as we are, by being tired or worn out, and Jesus promised them that he would restore a new rhythm to their lives and would show them how to 'live freely and lightly'. Life has a rhythm for each one of us, which is given to us by God to enable us to live each day in sync with his grace and love. Our task is to seek his will and then to align our lives with his purposes. This will inevitably involve a close scrutiny of our patterns of living, our workload in the office and the other activities that frequently disrupt our well-being and motivation. We may well have to cut out activities that are fruitless and cause us to be exhausted. Jesus' advice to us on the subject is compelling: 'Are you tired? Worn out? Burnt out on religion? Come to me. Get away with me and you'll recover your life. I'll show you how to take a real rest. Walk with me and work with me – watch how I do it. Learn the unforced rhythms of grace. I won't lay anything heavy or ill-fitting on you. Keep company with me and you'll learn to live freely and lightly' (Matthew 11:28–30, *The Message*).

I am a consultant psychiatrist and therefore am faced constantly with making difficult decisions at work. In the past I found it hard not to fall into doubt and self-reproach when things went wrong. I devised intricate tactics to cover this up but in my more private moments I thought that the fault lines in my personality would eventually split me into a thousand pieces, without hope of restoration (these times were my Humpty Dumpty moments).

In 1997, I began attending an Alpha course, because, uniquely for me, I had felt close to the end of life and no-one seemed to understand. Only a Christian friend was able to see through my defences and suggested I come to her Alpha group. I thought

'What the hell!' and knew I would be able to discern artificial or hysterical manifestations shown by others. I accepted the common sense wrapped up in Christian mumbo-jumbo as relatively harmless. At this time, I attended a weekend Christian conference on work-related issues. I was ready to go to the pub at the end of the proceedings, none the worse for spending two days in the company of Christians. There was an opportunity for prayer and I was happy to be able to sit with two friends who could pray harmlessly. I was quite surprised to be knocked back into my seat by a force that I identified immediately as passing through my 'cartoon' heart (i.e. not at the anatomical position closer to the centre of the chest). I was filled with an irrational sense of relief, followed by joy and then intense relaxation. I now realize this was the Holy Spirit.

At work, I tried to cap any behavioural changes in case anyone asked what was wrong. However, I was impressed by the perceptiveness of many friends and colleagues who said I was so much better, so much easier to be with and to work with. Someone asked what I was 'on' and where to get it. My ability to be seen as a supportive, trustworthy colleague and friend has increased. Both the clinical and academic areas of my work have benefited, with increased output of scientific papers and presentations at professional conferences. These are quantifiable results. What is even more striking, though more qualitative, is the way in which patients, relatives, and clinical colleagues respond to me. The most impressive changes have been internal. That nagging self-reproach that followed failure has all but gone.

I expected all of this to wear off like any fad, but several years later my sense of God's grace, love and immediacy is stronger than ever.

(Ken Checinski, consultant psychiatrist)

Recovering hope that has been impaired by failure is greatly helped when we realize that others can be helped by us. When we are going through rough times we do not believe that we can contribute anything to helping others to sort out their lives. This is not true. Often we are able to empathize far better with our colleagues who are under pressure at work when we too are finding life difficult. We do not need to have lives of perfect balance before we can be useful and see hope grow again. When we consciously lift our eyes above our own problems and become determined to encourage others we find that restoration is on its way.

In summary, hope is the forgotten virtue of our age, often sandwiched between the muscularity of faith and the tenderness of love. The world needs to know that God's plan is to sum up everything in Christ, and we are the ones through whom this hope will be made known now, in our workplaces and in the world. Hope is therefore powerful today, as it enables us to live in the present as it will be in the future. But we have trivialized hope to the point of whimsy. Radical hope looks at the reality of hard, difficult and sometimes impossible situations (which we encounter regularly at work) and without ignoring these realities empowers us in Christ to tackle them with confidence. That is the strength of the power of God at work. However, hope and perseverance go together. Without hope why persevere, why not live life for the moment or for immediate gain? But without perseverance hope falls at the first time of testing.

Archbishop Rowan Williams has called for a new 'culture of hope' for our nation. This is surely timely. Starting in our workplaces, all of us can share the passion to reverse the exhaustion of hopelessness that so saps the spiritual vitality of our workplaces and our nation.

I love the story of the first performance of Messiaen's 'Quartet for the End of Time'. In the winter of 1941, the composer Olivier Messiaen was one of a group of French prisoners of war in Stalag 8A in Silesia. He had read the Gospels and the book of Revelation and had come to believe that Jesus would return. He knew that this hope created meaning for the suffering people around him. In their appalling conditions, he understood that hope for tomorrow was essential for life today. He looked around the concentration camp and managed to gather together four instruments: a cello with a missing string, a battered violin, an old clarinet and a piano with stuck-together keys. For this unusual combination of broken instruments, he wrote one of the greatest pieces of music of the twentieth century, and Messiaen called it, 'Quartet for the End of Time'. When it was played to 5,000 prisoners of war in that freezing place in Silesia, the audience listened with rapt attention. Messiaen records, 'The cold was excruciating, the Stalag buried under snow, the four performers played on broken down instruments . . . But never have I had an audience who listened with such rapt attention and comprehension.' Those broken instruments in that unusual combination were unexpected agents of hope. Similarly, although we may feel inadequate and incomplete personally or spiritually, when we act together God uses us to be agents of hope in the world.

Money and Giving

For most of us, one of the results of our work is the monthly pay cheque. Of course money is not the only reward, but somehow money is viewed differently. We react sometimes positively and sometimes guiltily to receiving it. For the most part, we try not to talk about it. What impact does the money we earn have on our life? We need money to provide for our basic material needs, but does it also bring happiness? While most of us say that it doesn't, we feel deep down that a luxury holiday might just make all the difference. The magazines that uncover the lives of the rich and famous sell fast. Their trendsetting wardrobes, perfect children, sublime love lives and architect-designed homes fill the pages and influence our own goals. The desire for more money has crippled many with so-called 'affluenza' – the disease that can't stop wanting more. In his reflections on life, Guy de Rothschild said of money:

Everyone has it, no-one has enough. Reluctant to discuss it, they think of nothing else. People invest it with their own intimate feelings, their rivalries, their triumphs, their frustrations, their ambitions, their resentments. At night it grows into something real, overpowering, enlightening, protective, crushing. A phantasmagorical god . . . it was a means, it has become an end.

The prophet Haggai's description seems apt for our age: 'You eat, but never have enough. You drink, but never have your fill. You put on clothes, but are not warm. You earn wages, only to put them in a purse with holes in it' (Haggai 1:6).

Financial judgements are often impaired in this pursuit of more: people find themselves burdened by absurdly large mortgages or huge monthly credit card payments. The burdens of debt repayments turn money into a colossal weight, which can destroy. Credit was meant to facilitate the timing of purchases. It often becomes the fuel for our greed.

Excitement and status – can money deliver?

On a call-in programme on Capital Radio, the presenter asked the caller, 'What are you doing tonight?' He said, 'Oh, I'm bored.' 'Why are you bored?' asked the interviewer. 'I've got no money.' The caller's perception was that money would eradicate his boredom and provide excitement. Many of us put up with our week at work in anticipation of the weekend, or struggle through a year's work for the reward of a two-week holiday. Money, we believe, is a release from the grind of work.

Sir Nigel Rudd, the Chairman of Boots, when asked whether money motivated him, replied, 'Money buys you choices in life.' That is true, but which of these choices promote happiness? At a meeting with the head of a major European communications company, I looked out of the window to see his Bentley, in which he had been driven from his yacht that had sailed from his island home. 'These are not important to me,' he said. 'What is important is that they level the scores.' Money had given him status: his possessions had become the visible public benchmark of his performance against others.

Jesus or money – who will be master?

Jesus spent over half his teaching dealing with the subject of money and possessions. Many of his parables are about wealth, agriculture, business, debt forgiveness, and management performance – everyday examples of commerce. These teachings still form the basis for fulfilled living in a monied age. Jesus said, 'No servant can serve two masters. Either he will hate the one and love the other, or he will be devoted to the one and despise the other. You cannot serve both God and Money' (Luke 16:13). Words such as 'hate', 'love', 'despise' and 'devoted' are the normal words not of commercial language but of emotion and relationship. The key question is *with whom* will we have that relationship? Those who choose to serve God recognize him as master and keep money in its place. Those who don't, effectively choose money, and find that it masters them. Money, in this sense, is not purely nominal as economists would have it – a neutral basis for exchange – but numinous, powerful in itself. If money drives us, it tends to make us self-centred and crowds out other relationships. Our money-obsessed lives can spiral out of control. The amount of debt – both mortgages and consumer credit – that it is prudent to take on is a spiritual issue, not just an economic judgement.

Our approach to money and possessions is also a matter of geography. Jesus says, 'For where your treasure is, there your heart will be also' (Matthew 6:21). We therefore need to locate precisely, using the GPS of the Spirit, where our real 'treasure' lies. And treasure is simply what we value most in life. What do I really set my sights on and go after? But then we remember that Jesus set us the task in this world to build treasure in heaven. What does this mean? At its simplest, I believe we need to determine as a matter of fact what our driving motivations really are. If they are utterly selfish and materialist we need to correct them and build up acts and attitudes that are motivated by service to others. Storing up treasure in heaven (Matthew 6:20) becomes no more than the aggregation of daily acts of work well done, the proper use of money, activities undertaken in response to blessing others, and generosity when dealing with the needs of the people around us.

Our attitude to our finances is determined by a fundamental choice between God and money, not by our income bracket. Pay scales vary hugely in different fields and do not necessarily reflect the value or complexity of our work. You only need to contrast the income of a professional footballer with that of a nurse to bring this issue into sharp focus. The point here is what we do with what we have. I once spoke to a theology student on a tight grant. I was amazed by his greed in wanting more possessions. At around the same time I was deeply touched by speaking to the leader of a missionary youth group, whose personal circumstances were much the same as the student. He and his wife showed me their budget. I could not believe the degree of their generosity, particularly as they lived by the voluntary and uncertain contributions of others.

I recall a similar conversation sitting next to a billionaire on his private jet. I was appalled by his catalogue of acquisitive desires. He was hooked on greed. And yet after I had advised another multi-billionaire on the disposal of a major retail business for several billion dollars, I was staggered by the humility of his comments to me, the heavy responsibility he felt being entrusted with wealth and the total absence of greed.

In Luke 18, when Jesus meets the rich young ruler, he sees that his whole life is threatened because it is tied up in his 'great' wealth, and thus asks him to sell everything. The man goes away sad. But not everyone is called to sell everything. Indeed, in Proverbs 31, the woman is commended for setting about her work vigorously and ensuring that her trading is profitable. The story goes on with Jesus' comments on how hard it is for the rich to enter the kingdom. Commentators are divided on the precise meaning of 'It is easier for a camel to go through the eye of a needle than for a rich person to enter the kingdom of God' (Luke 18:25, *The Message*). Like many of the sayings of Jesus, it strikes me that he poses two utterly diverse images to make a similar point. It is impossible, not merely difficult, for a camel to go through the eye of a needle. Another interpretation points to a narrow pass outside Jerusalem through which a camel could only pass if what it was carrying was taken off to enable it to squeeze through. Either way, Jesus is clear that it would be impossible for a rich person to enter heaven. Are we therefore to conclude that heaven will be populated with the poor? Hence the despairing middle-class angst of those around him, probably still boat owners and prosperous fisherman, 'Who then can be saved?' Jesus replies, 'What is impossible with man is possible with God' (Luke 18:27).

Following Christ in the world today is not just difficult, it is impossible. To do so we need God's help. He alone can turn the apparently impossible requirements for living righteously in a hostile world into the entirely possible way of life for Christ's followers.

But Peter's reaction was one of indignation. 'We have left everything to follow you! What then will there be for us?' (Matthew 19:27). We can relate to his reaction. How often do we assess situations, projects or friendships with the unexpressed, 'What's in it for me?' question? The honest question of self-interest enables Jesus to give his assurance: everyone who has put him first in their relationships and in their possessions will receive 100 times as much in this world and will inherit far more in the next (Matthew 19:29).

We should expect fair compensation for a job well done, and should thus be confident yet gracious about conducting salary negotiations and asking for appropriate pay rises. Jesus makes it quite clear that 'the worker deserves his wages' (Luke 10:7). And Paul reinforces this message when he underlines, in three images, his passionate belief in the merits of reward for hard work. He mentions the soldiers of the day. They were mercenaries and therefore properly entitled to be paid. He goes on to ask rhetorically, 'Who plants a vineyard and does not eat of its grapes? Who tends a flock and does not drink of the milk?' (1 Corinthians 9:7). He is emphatic: 'When the ploughman ploughs and the thresher threshes, they ought to do so in the hope of sharing in the harvest' (1 Corinthians 9:10). It is not possible to be effective in the workplace without a degree of personal motivation, which will involve setting targets and being rewarded for our achievements. But radical choices have to be made if our relationship with money threatens our relationship with God. Money is not evil in itself, but the lust for money is a root of all kinds of evil, trapping us in harmful desires and ultimately bringing about our ruin (1 Timothy 6:9–10).

Greed or generosity – how do we deal with money?

Jesus had a special concern for the marginalized and the poor. But he also ate with the rich and privileged (Luke 11:37; Luke 14:1), enjoyed the wedding feast at Cana (John 2:1) and accepted, without demurring, the anointing with costly perfume (Matthew 26:7). He lived passionately at both ends of the human scale, not midway in a guilty compromise.

When Fi and I got married, the central theme of our

marriage service was John 10:10: 'I have come that they may have life, and have it to the full.' We are called to the good life, but this can only be enjoyed in relationship with God and others. In this way, we need not be defensive about enjoying the financial rewards of work.

We should aim to develop Paul's ability to be contented in times of plenty and in times of need (Philippians 4:11–12). God may bless us with money, but it is not necessarily evidence of his favour.

Martin Luther said, 'There are three conversions necessary: the conversion of the heart, mind, and the purse.' When Zacchaeus met Jesus, he made an immediate public declaration, straightening out his finances, giving half his money to the poor and paying back anyone he had cheated four times the amount. Jesus told him, 'Today salvation has come to this house' (Luke 19:9). When we sort out our financial affairs we become open to the blessings of a full life lived as God intended. This is not a one-off event, but an ongoing way of living.

I am always struck by Jesus' comments on money in Luke 16:10–11. First, if you handle small amounts of money properly, then you can be trusted with large sums. But if you cut corners on small things – the VAT fiddle or cheating on the bus fare – then who will trust you in big things (Luke 16:10)? Second, if you cannot handle money properly, who will trust you with true riches (Luke

16:11)? The test is in small things. Small ways in which we use our money determine the trust that can be placed in us not only by other people but by God. I often remind myself when I long for a deeper spiritual relationship with God to start with the small things, for example, handling money with integrity. The material and spiritual run together in maturing a good relationship with God.

The capitalist economy relies on holding money tightly. Christ's economy is different. Hoarding resources may well inflate a bank account but will not bring with it the joy that grows out of regular giving. In some extraordinary way I have found that the more I have given the greater have been God's blessings. That is the testimony of many Christians.

Duty and privilege – why do we give?

Giving belongs not to the suburbs of Christianity but to the very centre of our spiritual lives. Giving is spirituality made real. Few people naturally give away their hardearned money – it is the example of God's grace that gives us both the desire and the ability to be generous. Sometimes it is not a straight choice between keeping our money for ourselves or giving it away. Our investment decisions can take into account not just our own return, but additional factors such as giving a friend a business opportunity or a place to live.

One of the ways in which we get distracted from giving is when our fear of financial insecurity overwhelms a God-given desire to be generous. This is a straightforward challenge to all of us. Will we live by faith, or by fear? Giving is not simply a financial transaction. It is essentially an act of trust in an economic order that goes against the grain of the modern world view. There is a struggle for supremacy between these two polarities. We clearly need to be wise and not headstrong. Not every need can be satisfied by us. We therefore need to be judicious in striking a balance between known commitments and the desire for spontaneous giving.

When the psalmist says he will honour God 'above all gods' (Psalm 96:4), he is not merely stating the obvious but making it plain that there is a competitive struggle for ascendancy in our lives that goes on between the true God and the various pretenders – money, security, fulfilment. He has made a deliberate choice and has chosen the living God. We too make choices that are neither easy nor painless.

Generous regular giving is one of the ways in which we underline to the spiritual powers that attempt to draw us away from God that we trust in him and his control of all our resources. It is a venture of faith and therefore will be

subject to attack: money can become an obstacle or a gateway to God's blessing. Giving is one of the great privileges
we have and a practical way of responding to God's love.
When we get our giving right the wonderful promise of
God is this: 'Test me in this and see if I don't open up
heaven itself to you and pour out blessings beyond your
wildest dreams' (Malachi 3:10, *The Message*).

1. Celebration

Giving is a form of worshipping God, celebrating his
goodness and enjoying what we have. We have received
blessings from him – there is no better way to respond
than to be generous to others. As we thank God by being
generous, it seems that our thanks can be multiplied. Paul,
writing to encourage generosity in the Christians at
Corinth, says, 'Because of the service by which you have
proved yourselves, [people] will praise God' (2 Corinthians 9:13). God loves a cheerful giver (2 Corinthians 9:7).
He wants to see the smile on our faces when we give. At
the church where I worship we have Gift Days when we
restate our vision and ask the congregation to contribute.
Sandy Millar, former vicar of Holy Trinity Brompton, who
initiated this way of giving, urged us to indulge only in
'hilarious giving', saying, 'If you can't give with a smile,
don't give at all!' Thus we make an effort to accentuate the
joy of giving by having a carnival atmosphere, with accom-

panying music and singing as people come up to the front of the church to put their pledges into a basket. This is a deliberate liturgy which is founded in the belief that God wishes our giving to be festive rather than sullen. This joyful overflowing has spiritual significance, challenging our assumptions that giving is always covert and painful.

2. Freedom

Generous giving is liberating. Every time we give, we issue a defiant statement to the forces that lie behind money, saying in effect, 'You don't have a hold on me.' Wealth can give us the illusion of independence from God. As we grow more affluent the temptation is to put our security in our possessions and to grow less dependent on God. By doing so, we begin to choke the life of the Spirit. Giving in the power of the Spirit is the best way that I know of breaking the potential grip of money and of keeping it in its rightful place. What we cannot give freely, possesses us. Giving is the antidote to materialism.

3. Investment

My father was a farmer. When I watched him planting orange trees, I would say to him, 'But it's going to take such a long time to get fruit.' However, he was looking ahead to the harvest. He even developed a method of planting two trees next to each other in order to increase the harvest. Giving is our planting and the harvest is our righteousness (2 Corinthians 9:10). Giving is a central part of the process by which we become more like Christ – the aim of every believer. A wise pastor once asked me the disarming questions: 'How Christ-like are you today? How's your giving?' Being Christ-like is inseparable from giving. As we give generously today we do so not only to alleviate immediate need but also as an investment for future generations.

In Paul's teaching on giving in 2 Corinthians, he says: 'Whoever sows sparingly will also reap sparingly, and whoever sows generously will also reap generously' (2 Corinthians 9:6). This echoes Jesus' own words: 'Give, and it will be given to you . . . For with the measure you use, it will be measured to you' (Luke 6:38). Not pound sterling for pound sterling, but blessing upon blessing. God doesn't necessarily promise us financial prosperity but he does promise to supply all our needs and he does assure us of an ongoing relationship with him that lasts into eternity.

When we give, we are not only investing in our own relationship with God, but also in God's wider kingdom.

My local church called an emergency meeting regarding funding. It seemed that we'd over-extended ourselves in our evangelistic activities and we either needed to cut back or find a significant sum of money. As the discussion progressed, it dawned on me that we were in a very privileged position, as we were starting to see some exciting results. Other generations would have given anything for this. I realized that giving was an investment in the kingdom, not just a drain on our bank accounts. After the meeting, it was amazing to see all the money that we needed coming in from a variety of sources.

(Tom Johnson, City analyst)

Paul is clear that the giving of the Philippians is a credit to their account (Philippians 4:17–18). We have personal investment accounts that only God audits. But we should not forget that our giving is not a debit on the account but a credit. True, when we give we deduct from our bank accounts, but then immediately a credit is posted in the portfolio of investment in God's kingdom. One day the audit report will be read. It is a salutary question to ask, 'Will I dread it like a bad school report, or wait eagerly for the master's, "Well done"?'

Who, how, when, what? – the practicalities of giving

Giving is a work of God's grace in our lives. So we can ask God to help us to want to give. Then we just start. I regret how long it took me to establish a good life pattern of giving. Even now it's not perfect. There are always reasons, none of them good, for putting this off. Start small – start by giving money to people, causes, objectives that you feel strongly about. But just start! Giving is a habit that, once established, brings huge benefits.

Who?

It is important to think carefully and pray about the individual or organization we are proposing to give to. Once my wife and I have decided on the total amount it is right to give, we slice the cake in a fairly disciplined manner. The lion's share goes to our church. We trust the leadership to use the money wisely and feel responsible as congregation members both to help pay for boring running costs (such as heating, lighting and administration) and to contribute to the church's vision. The next slice goes to other local or global Christian organizations that attract us personally. We are particularly keen to support evangelism before general charitable giving, as these wider initiatives have a much bigger potential pool of donors. In one sense we treat our giving like any other investment and make a point of listening to our 'investment reports' (also known as missionary feedback). We find it very encouraging when we recognize in the lives changed the yield on our money and prayers. Paul, writing to the Philippians, thanked them for sharing in his financial troubles (Philippians 4:15). Giving cements a relationship with those who receive and gives us the opportunity to remain involved in their lives.

Although most of our giving is planned, if someone on the street asks me for money, I usually give, largely as a ministry to myself. Some people object that they will just get their next fix. Perhaps, perhaps not. But it is a constant reminder of how difficult it is to part with money and how generous God is. However small the amount, it builds a sustainable pattern of generosity.

How?

The Pharisees wanted others to see their giving and they were rebuked for their ostentation. Some giving should be anonymous – the left hand not knowing what the right hand is doing (Matthew 6:3). On other occasions, it is right to make clear the source of the gift. This is not to invite a debtor relationship. Rather, it is to demonstrate the body of Christ working to meet each other's needs. Christ is honoured when the known needs of Christians are met by other Christians.

Five years ago we unexpectedly found ourselves unable to pay our daughter's school fees. Before we'd even had a chance to panic, a couple that we vaguely knew from church sent us a cheque to cover the whole year, giving us enough time to sort ourselves out financially. Recently we found out that another couple at our children's school were in a similar situation. We were only able to cover a term for them, but giving has never been so enjoyable!

(Lisa Gray, production assistant)

There are many ways to give.

As a nurse, I accept that my shift patterns sometimes involve working over the weekend. However, wherever possible, I request Sundays off so that I can help with the church youth group. I've decided that this is a priority – so it's worth forfeiting the enhanced Sunday rate.

(Becs Harris, staff nurse)

We can also give our skills, time and energy, or share our possessions. If we have a spare room in our home that could provide accommodation, we can offer it. If we have a garden, we can let others enjoy it. If we have a car, we can insure someone else to drive it. At all times, we need to be wise about sharing, setting limits to avoid abuse and to protect our families.

When?

There is undoubtedly a blessing that comes from regular giving. 'On the first day of every week, each one of you should set aside a sum of money in keeping with your income' (1 Corinthians 16:2). Whenever our money comes in, we should set aside a sum proportionate to what we are earning. This should be the first, rather than the last, deduction. Like many other payments, such as mortgages or credit cards, giving regularly is best. Impulse giving is good but not sufficient. We need to plan the bulk of our giving while leaving room for moments of spontaneous generosity.

What?

In the New Testament we are not told the precise amount that we should give. At one level, this is strange. Both Jesus and Paul had ample opportunity to reinforce the tithe message. Paul could of course have assumed it in his teaching on financial giving, but perhaps 'the apostle of the free spirit' was making a wider and more momentous point by his silence: generosity is not quantifiable. Instead, most of the teaching focuses on our attitude. It is inconceivable to Jesus that we should have a loving heart and not show this by our actions. 'You give a tenth of your spices . . . But you have neglected the more important matters of the law – justice, mercy and faithfulness. You should have practised the latter, without neglecting the former' (Matthew 23:23). There is a hint here that a tithe (the ten per cent) is taken for granted: but equally this is a passage not on tithing but on attitudes and transparency.

I am often asked about tithes. Behind the question is partly a desire for a biblical view but also the longing for certainty. I believe that although the prescriptive rules on tithing were appropriate for a non-welfare state economy in Old and New Testament times, they remain a good practical guide for giving today. Of course, if our salaries increase, we should revise our giving upwards, always aiming to be generous and not duty-bound.

Giving inevitably brings about a drop in our standard of living. Anybody who gives generously will have less for other material things but will find their lives greatly enriched.

At times people get into a mess financially and find themselves in debt. By debt, I am not referring to long-term prudent mortgage repayments, which are a normal part of people's lives. So what do we do about giving if we are in financial crisis? I believe that getting out of debt as quickly as possible is the best way to honour God. I would advise talking to someone trustworthy in order first to acknowledge the problem, and second to establish a credible plan to resolve it. In the short-term, everything other than true essentials should be suspended. I would only suspend giving temporarily – as part of a programme of quite drastic lifestyle cutbacks – and would never stop giving without knowing when I planned to start again. It can also be helpful to mark the fact that we are back on track financially and free to be generous with our money again with a one-off celebratory donation.

I think it is important to talk about money, but we need to do so carefully and sensitively, choosing the right people. When I was trying to establish a healthy pattern of giving I talked regularly with one friend who I felt understood my situation. I trusted him and found his calm and steady manner particularly reassuring.

What then, in summary, should be our attitude to money? Is it filthy lucre which will contaminate us, or is it a force for good? Of its own it is neither: it is our attitude to its use that will govern which it is to be. That is why thankful, regular and cheerful giving is so important. Not only does it honour God's name but expectant giving enables us to rely on God's promise to 'supply all your needs according to his glorious riches in Christ Jesus' (Philippians 4:19). The net result is that we experience the freedom to enjoy our possessions, our money, our holidays, our gadgets and cars. Giving frees us up to enjoy God's goodness precisely because our priorities are right as we provide first for the needs of others and then for ourselves.

God, 'who richly provides us with everything for our enjoyment', also tells us to be 'willing to share' (1 Timothy 6:17–18). There is therefore every good reason for us to enjoy material benefits in proportion to the way we live, the generosity of our giving and our gratitude to God, the provider. This attitude leads to the responsible enjoyment of our possessions. A good indication that we have the balance right is that we are able to enjoy both what we have and what we give.

There is, as ever, much practical wisdom in Proverbs on the subject of money and possessions. Proverbs 23:4 is a reminder to all of us: 'Do not wear yourself out to get rich; have the wisdom to show restraint. Cast but a glance at riches, and they are gone, for they will surely sprout wings and fly off to the sky like an eagle.'

In conclusion, it is worth looking at an extract from John Wesley's brilliant sermon, *The Use of Money.*

Gain all you can, without hurting either yourself or your neighbour, in soul or body, by applying hereto with unintermitted diligence, and with all the understanding which God has given you; save all you can, by cutting off every expense which serves only to indulge foolish desire, to gratify either the desire of the flesh, the desire of the eye, or the pride of life; waste nothing, living or dying, on sin or folly, whether for yourself or your children; and then, give all you can, or, in other words, give all you have to God. Do not stint yourself . . . to this or that proportion. Render unto God, not a tenth, not a third, not half, but all that is God's, be it more or less; by employing all on yourself, your household, the household of faith and all mankind, in such a manner, that you may give a good account of your stewardship, when ye can be no longer stewards.

Spiritual Renewal

Vicente Fox, while President of Mexico, addressed a gathering of business and political leaders at the World Economic Forum with these words:

> No aspect of contemporary life is more notable and less understood than the spiritual discontent and restlessness that is spreading worldwide. This unease is present among those who are safe and wealthy as well as among the poor and desperate. We can now see throughout the world a rejection of crass materialism and an intense undirected desire for spiritual rebirth.

Finding meaning and purpose in life is, I believe, the greatest challenge of our time. This search is as essential to establishing lasting peace, sustainable economic activity and strong communities at ease with each other as any of the other major challenges of climate change, elimination of extreme poverty or globalization.

Fox described the desire for renewal as 'intense'. I believe he is right. There is a new intensity in the search for values and a meaningful way of life. The surge in spiritual hunger, particularly among young people, has increased, and the institutional church has largely found itself unable to provide the necessary food. So many people's search continues without guidance – 'undirected'. Within the church, the 'official guides' are taken up in a distracting internal agenda of their own relating to the role of women, sexuality and other parochial agendas, debates that seem irrelevant to most. For many, therefore, this undirected search merely leads into the dead ends of contemporary fads.

At the end of 2005 Her Majesty the Queen addressed the General Synod of the Church of England and reminded us of this hunger for meaning in the knowledge society.

> When so much is in flux, when limitless amounts of information, much of it ephemeral, are instantly accessible on demand, there is a renewed hunger for that which endures and gives meaning. The Christian church can speak uniquely to that need, for at the heart of our faith stands the conviction that all people, irrespective of race, background or circumstances, can find lasting significance and purpose in the gospel of Jesus Christ.

I have written this book from a Christian point of view at a time when there is global resurgence of faith not confined to Christianity. Every boardroom, workplace and community will therefore have to grapple with the challenges of respect for different faiths and inter-faith dialogue if they are to respond positively to this world-wide phenomenon. Faith, far from being a delusion, capable of being dismissed as irrelevant to the modern workplace, will increasingly become a value to be nurtured as enlightened corporations rightly accentuate the importance of diversity at work.

The truth is that God is at work in his world. He is shaking and shaping its future. We remember the words of the 'Our Father', which reminds that his will is done *on earth* as it is in heaven. 'Earth' comes first – I believe deliberately, as a reminder of our priorities to be rooted in this world. He has chosen us to show that 'spirituality' starts with God, and has a clear mission: to bring healing and restoration to a fragmented society. He does so by holding together all our activities. I am repeatedly struck by the understanding that the Lord of compassion is also the Lord of commerce; the Lord of prayer is also the Lord of profit; and the Lord of mission is also the Lord of the money markets. He takes charge of the whole of creation and of all our endeavours. Finding spiritual renewal in a relationship with him is the key to fulfilled living but only comes when we recognise that wisdom starts with God. Wisdom is his unique spirituality for the world.

How do we recognize God at work in us? Irenaeus, the early church leader, said, 'The glory of God is a human being fully alive'. Are we fully alive to God, willing to be moulded by the Holy Spirit?

Michael Caine was once asked to differentiate between a movie star and a great movie actor. His reply was instructive: 'The movie star says, "How can I change the script and story line to fit my personality?" The great actor says, "How can I change my personality to fit the script and to do justice to the story?"' If we want to be written into God's script for the world, we need to be prepared to change. We need to be willing to yield our programmes to his priorities. We need a spirituality that is neither rigid nor static, nor compartmentalized, but that grows and deepens into every aspect of our lives, bringing profound inner peace. Such connectedness distinguishes Christian spirituality from other efforts at calm and peace. God is always at work, changing us, if we let him do so. He is committed to work in us, only through us. He is not the control freak chief executive. In the film *Junebug*, the wife turns to her husband and says, 'God loves you just the way you are, but he loves you too much to let you stay that way.' As a contemporary summary of theology this sentence is unbeatable.

Many questions are raised by faith and spirituality. But there is evidence that faith is growing. This augurs well for the future. I recently had lunch with a chairman of a large listed company. At the end of lunch, he turned to me and said that he had been reviewing his life. There were several boxes. The first was work and he felt – rightly in my view – that he had been a success. The second was his family relationships. He had been divorced and he had made a special effort to ensure that his relationships with the children of his first marriage and his new family were good. This had not been easy but he felt that this was a part of his life under control. Another box he marked 'friendships'. During the last year he had paid particular attention to his friends, especially those who in the ceaseless demands of the workplace might have been neglected. He felt enriched by these efforts to rekindle these friendships from university and elsewhere.

Then he turned to me and said, 'But there is one box that is unfilled. I don't know what to call it. But it would have something to do with the spiritual. I need to make sense of this non-material aspect of my life as I suspect it will give a key to a fuller meaning to the other parts of my life. Somehow this is the missing part of my life.'

Connectivity is one of the great drivers of modern technology. This is demonstrated by the speed with which computers can talk to each other and data can be carried.

Similarly the Holy Spirit is the connector, the fluid and frictionless link between humanity and its Creator.

We all know the frustration of losing the connection when we are online, and the delight of broadband keeping us linked in. In earlier translations of John's Gospel, Jesus calls us to 'Abide in me' (John 15:4, ESV). 'Staying connected' might be the modern translation. A true connectedness to God is the secret of successful living in the workplace, and will transform our relationships at work. The starting point is not our religion but our common humanity – precisely the point of God's connection with us through the Incarnation. If we demonstrate that we are completely and sacrificially 'for' our colleagues, perhaps Christians will cease to be known for what they are against.

As Christians, we are, in a wider sense, for society and not against it. We are called to be part of a wider social and moral order that is worth fighting for and defending. The prevailing structure is based on an atomized view of life, which celebrates an individualistic ethic, demonstrated by the widespread pursuit of possessions. But to seek riches without caring for others is ultimately to experience poverty. We are impoverished whenever the wider interests of humanity are excluded from our day-to-day working lives. The 'Make Poverty History' campaign was crucial to our age: we cannot live in a world of extreme poverty and not wish to act to redress this injustice.

There is a haunting judgement in Malachi 2:2 in which God says to the people of Israel that if they disregard his ways '[he] will curse [their] blessings'. We see each day the tragic consequences of the way we have inflicted this judgement upon ourselves. We are prosperous, yet our family life is fragmenting before our very eyes. We have a chronic fear of the future. We are frightened in our streets as crimes against the person grow and in a myriad of ways we see the tapestry of our society torn beyond recognition by the unrestrained forces of consumerism, greed and envy. How do we weave back into the tapestry the broken threads that once again could illustrate a true picture of God reflected in our places of work and the society around us?

The answer to these questions lies in a new discovery of radical hardcore Christianity – a faith that has been stripped to its essentials. The Holy Spirit who reminds the world of its need for God (John 16:8) is not only the instrument of judgement but also the binding agent who links our lives at work to a greater social movement that we call the kingdom of God, and which we long to see taking root on earth.

This movement underpins the communities in which we work, regards the stability that comes from family life as the first building block for a sustained society, accepts accountability in public affairs as essential for the economy to flourish, and yet hears the cries of the marginalized, the poor and disadvantaged and takes seriously all efforts to eradicate the extremes of global poverty. This is a movement that is not based on muddle-headed economics but has the true ingredients of a productive and compassionate social order that most closely reflects the true freedom of the New Testament.

This is a movement that could close society's 'gaps'. For example, in the UK over 70 per cent of people believe in God, but few of these enjoy the benefits of being active followers. How can we narrow this gap when we have failed to provide an attractive model for living authentic Christian lives? How can we eradicate the distinction between sacred and secular, which has created such a harmful passivity among Christians? How can we narrow the gap between extreme poverty and rich nations, between domestic protection and global free trade, and between those who hope in God and those who live without hope?

Bridging these gaps is a Trinitarian imperative. God embraced those who were anti-God because he wished to close the gap that had arisen between the vitality of the Godhead, reflected in the first Creation, and the miserable lives lived by those who turned from him. God was interested in community well before he became interested in the church.

The task is so immense that nothing short of a new Pentecost, an outpouring of the Spirit that brings newness, creativity and adventure, is required if we are to see our places of work transformed, our communities throbbing with life, and our society healed. Herein lies true prosperity. We cannot achieve much on our own and will become dispirited, but with the Holy Spirit there is enormous power.

I thank God for the privilege of living as a witness for him at the start of the twenty-first century. I would wish to live at no other time in history – not even in Judea at the time of Jesus. Opportunities for spreading the good news have never been greater. The real economic cost of travel and communication is declining year by year. The message does not have to be contained geographically or through lack of communication. Modern technology makes it possible to spread the good news more effectively than ever before. The challenge will be to ensure that we can use the advantages of modern technology to execute a coherent strategy for returning the workplace to its roots of faith-based values. Close observation of chief executives of global corporations shows that they fail not because of a lack of vision, but for a lack of delivering results. Getting things done is one of the great requirements of success in modern business. This is also true of the church, and ordinary Christians need to get on with the job of transforming the workplace and the nation. This is central to our mission to the world. The task of recovering a whole-of-life faith is not one that can be delegated to bishops and church leaders. At a time of crisis in the church, a fresh lay initiative is needed to reconnect the workplace with Christianity. There are enormous spiritual and economic benefits to be gained from restoring purpose and value to our workplaces. We can easily work in not-for-profit organizations: we cannot however work in not-for-purpose organizations. If we are not convinced of the purpose of our work we will never work well and enjoy it.

The last book that Pope John Paul II wrote before he died was a reflection of Jesus' call of John 14:31: 'Get up. Let's go. It's time to leave here' (*The Message* version). We are all on a journey and we will not be able to locate every point on the map. We are utterly reliant on the Holy Spirit to show us the way. We do not have any fear of the world because of Jesus' promise: 'Take heart! I have overcome the world' (John 16:33). The task is enormous but the promise of fulfilled living and the restoration of the values with which God started our world is a huge prize. We will never make any progress without recognizing that we are sustained by his grace. If we are to see our society truly transformed and our nation turned to God, it will only come about when the people at work rise to this vision. We are the unseen army of connectors touching millions of people each day. As we re-engage with people at work we could see a viral explosion of faith. The missionary effect of Christians at work living authentic lives, weak yet empowered by the Holy Spirit, vulnerable yet strengthened by God, anxious yet filled with peace, could, through a new outpouring of God's Spirit, become the greatest evangelistic movement of our age.